D0175638

The Burden of Support

The Burden of Support
Young Latinos in an Aging Society

David E. Hayes-Bautista, Werner O. Schink, and
Jorge Chapa

Stanford University Press, Stanford, California

Stanford University Press
Stanford, California
© 1988 by the Board of Trustees of the
Leland Stanford Junior University
Printed in the United States of America
Original printing 1988
Last figure below indicates year of this printing:
99 98 97 96 95 94 93 92 91 90

CIP data appear at the end of the book

To
Maria, Catalina, and Diego Hayes-Bautista
Pat, Sonia, and Louis Schink
and
Belinda De La Rosa

Preface

Contemporary America is undergoing massive demographic and economic changes. Our society is currently riding on a large wave of Baby Boom prosperity and productivity. This population group will retire in the beginning of the twenty-first century. Whether or not our society remains competitive in the world economy at that time hinges directly on the productivity of the generation that will follow the Baby Boomers. In California and many other states, this generation will be largely composed of minorities, especially Latinos. In order to respond to these changes our political leadership must take a long-term view.

Our society is undergoing demographic changes in the racial, ethnic, and sex composition of three major age groups—youth, workers, and the elderly. These changes may well be the most important social trend in the United States over the next fifty years. Understanding these changes is fundamental to charting a successful course for American society.

The bulk of the book deals with Latino demographic, social, and economic characteristics: labor force participation, income, education, health, and political participation. In order to improve their situation, Latinos must understand their position as a group and as a community. The non-Latino population must become aware that this improvement of Latino status is also to its benefit. Latinos are underrepresented in many basic social roles, show low rates of political participation and economic productivity, and have a limited sense of commitment and belonging. There is a clear opportunity for developing and expanding our Latino intellectual traditions, particularly as they pertain to Latino social policy research. The Latino community needs to better understand itself and its role in society. It needs to make the rest of society understand itself as well.

Other minorities similarly need to understand themselves and each other in terms of similarities and differences for the optimal political, economic, and social outcome. For example, strong similarities of interest exist in the area of immigration policies between Latinos and many Asian groups. Of concern here are issues of bilingualism, biculturalism, and access to employment, health care, and education. Blacks and Latinos share the common misfortune of high dropout rates, low income, and low occupational status.

The Anglo population currently occupies a position of economic and political leadership in our society. Anglos must realize that their future economic well-being hinges on the productivity of a largely non-Anglo work force.

It is quite likely that many members of the Anglo population, i.e., white non-Latinos, will be unfamiliar and perhaps uncomfortable with the label Anglo. They may think that this inaccurately represents their ancestry and identity. This may indicate to them how many Latinos feel about being labeled Hispanic. The term Latino applies to people of Mexican, Caribbean, and Central and South American origin or ancestry, and is an aggregate of several distinct groups of different national origin. In California, the social, economic, and demographic characteristics of the different Latino national-origin groups are sufficiently similar to use one label for all.

Although this book's point of departure is California's demographic future, the problems and issues discussed here are not limited to California. Fully 10 percent of the U.S. population currently resides in California. The entire nation will experience similar age and ethnic shifts, with the effects particularly felt in several states and many large urban areas. Although there are some uncertainties in any projection of the future, the basic trends are clear. The Anglo Baby Boomers will retire in the early part of the twenty-first century, and our work force will become far more dependent on the skills and productivity of Latinos and other minorities.

This book, although conceived, elaborated, and written by the three of us, has its roots in our connections with the world around us. Various people, at different times, have assisted our work in diverse manners, and we should like to acknowledge them here.

Douglas X. Patino, while he was Secretary of the California Health and Welfare Agency, had the foresight to introduce two of us (Hayes-Bautista and Schink) to each other, and to ask us to prepare an initial set of demographic projections for the California Hispanic Affairs Council, which was published as *The Hispanic Portfolio* (1982). During the preparation of that short monograph, the third member of our team (Chapa), through his work with the California Health and Welfare Agency, came on board. As work progressed on what was to become this manuscript, Stanford University Press and its Editor, J. G. Bell, in particular, became quite interested in the basic concept. After meeting with us and encouraging us, he promptly retired (we hope there was no correlation), delivering us into the capable hands of Bill Carver. After the manuscript was complete, it was given to our editor, Barbara Mnookin, who wore down numerous red pencils organizing our sociological policy jargon into a fair imitation of the English language.

As we prepared data, we were fortunate to have the cooperation of many people and many agencies: Vincent Torres-Gil and Gwendolyn Dobbert of the California Department of Health Statistics; Dr. Javier Garcia de Alba of the Universidad de Guadalajara, who opened his data files and his home to us; the Chicano Studies Library at the University of California, Berkeley; and the Chicano Studies Research Center Library at UCLA.

As portions of the book were written, many people took time from their busy schedules to read and comment on it, including Jorge Bustamante of the Colegio de la Frontera, Tijuana, B.C.; Dr. Garcia de Alba, Osmar Matsui, Raul Padilla, and Margarita Sierra of the Universidad de Guadalajara; Henrick Blum, Ivan Jaksic, Joan Bloom, Richard Scheffler, Auristela Perez, Sylvia Guendelman, Joel Garcia, Andres Jimenez, Alex Saragoza, and Meredith Minkler of the University of California, Berkeley; Fernando Torres-Gil and Abraham Lowenthal of the University of Southern California; Jaime Rodriguez of the University of California, Irvine; Arturo Gomez-Pompa and Kathy Roberts of the University of California, Riverside; Paul Ong of the University of California, Los Angeles; David Sanchez of the University of California, San Francisco; and the *cuates* of the Chicano Studies Research Center at UCLA—Victor Becerra, Antonio Serrata, Maria Cuevas, Anthony Hernandez, Lupe Gonzales, Bill de la Torre, Marta Gonzalez, Mike Soldatenko, Ruth Zambrana, Robert Valdez, Rina Alcalay, Richard Chabran, Nelly Salgado, Richard Cervantes, Juan Lara, Linda Avila, Blanca Chavoya, Ray Paredes, and Robert Montoya.

Additionally, support was provided by *el jefe*, Ruben Rodriguez, and his wife Socorro, Roberto and Catalina Rodarte, Patricio and Adriana Mijares, Raul and Ana Bracamontes, Tita (Marta Ynez), Quel (Ana Raquel), Jon and Avril Stewart, Peter Yedidia, Connie Rubiano, Margarita and Felipe Paredes, Roberto and Van McGee, and Margarito Bautista.

The secretarial assistance of Emily Wright, Barbara Martin, Maria Ortiz, Ada Arensdorf, and Olga Barrios is gratefully acknowledged. The in-kind support proffered by the UCLA Chicano Studies Research Center is also gratefully acknowledged.

D.H-B.
W.O.S.
J.C.

Contents

Tables

*

Text

Appendix

xiv   *Tables*

Figures

Foreword

Based on my own experience as a policy maker in two state governments, I strongly adhere to the principle that good policy evolves from careful, thorough analysis; that all good planning is based on an assessment of the future; that formal, systematic simulations with a clear presentation of assumptions are preferred to ad hoc, implicit projections of the future; and that the evaluation of a variety of alternatives is preferred over the consideration of only one possibility. *The Burden of Support* presents a set of systematic projections, as well as a well-reasoned analysis of issues, which are critical to policy makers in determining whether the future of our society will be interdependent and productive or segmented and non-productive.

The pioneering aspects of *The Burden of Support* should be not only noted but appreciated. During my tenure as the California Secretary of Health and Welfare, I was alarmed that there were no demographic projections of the Latino population available. As a policy maker I was keenly aware of the needs for such projections. The earliest projections by the authors were presented in a widely read monograph, *The Hispanic Portfolio*, published by the California Hispanic Affairs Council. *The Burden of Support* evolved from the earlier work, with many refinements and enhancements. (The point of departure is California's demographic future.) Although there are uncertainties in any projection of the future, the basic trends are clear. The Anglo baby boomers will retire in the early part of the twenty-first century, and our work force will become far more dependent on the skills and productivity of Latinos and other minorities. This book is the most comprehensive and systematic treatise on this topic available. It reflects the authors' dedication, sophistication, and commitment not only to good public policy, but to the public good.

Comprendalo bien!

Douglas X. Patino

The Burden of Support

Chapter One

California in 2030:
The Worst-Case Scenario

In the same way that a physical model of a bridge provides a testing ground for different combinations of design and materials, a scenario allows us to model society in the future. We offer here some grounded speculation about the future of society, given two very important trends occurring simultaneously: the aging of the well-educated, Anglo Baby Boom generation; and the growth of the much younger, less-educated Latino population. The worst-case scenario below is designed to be extreme.

The Scenario

By 1995 the growth of the Latino population in California was viewed with growing concern by the Anglo population. Spreading out from such areas of concentration as East Los Angeles, East San Jose, South San Diego, central Orange County, and the Mission District of San Francisco, Latino communities began to overflow into and then absorb many previously Anglo areas. Residential suburbs "turned" almost overnight, as Anglo homeowners left in a near-panic, hoping to sell their houses before a general property devaluation set in. New suburbs were pushed farther away from the city cores, requiring both the conversion of agricultural land and virgin desert to residential use and the development of increasingly elaborate systems to provide transportation and water to these areas far removed from the decaying cores.

Meanwhile, the graying of the Anglo population continued, with the number of elderly climbing steadily but slowly after 1985 until 2010, when the Baby Boom generation began to turn 65. Thereafter, the number of elderly increased rapidly. The pool of Social Security recipients nearly doubled between 1990 and 2020. The Medicare program saw a tremendous increase in its beneficiaries. Much of the attention in health care shifted to providing expensive services to these people. Hospitals that catered to the elderly sprang up, eager to take advantage of the fact that their illnesses were chronic, needing attention over a long period of time. Indeed, the medical-care industry was in a growth mode from 1995 until about 2015, expanding services and structures on the projected volume of business the growth of the elderly population would bring.

By 1995 most Californians had become aware that Latinos were the single largest group enrolled in public schools. This had two effects. First, it accelerated the "white flight" away from public schools and into private schools. And second, since fewer and fewer Anglo children were being born, a trend that had started at least a decade earlier, educational issues had long since ceased being a priority for the Anglo population. Bond issues to replace decaying, and at times dangerous, facilities were routinely defeated, and there was an increasing clamor from the electorate to reduce overall expenditures in education. If there were few Anglo children of school age and if most of those were enrolled in private schools, so the argument went, why should the Anglo population be taxed for services that it was not using? Beginning in 1995 revenues for schools began to be cut drastically. After 2010 they were cut still more drastically, as the state began to develop programs to make up for the deficiencies in the federal Social Security and Medicare systems and private pension plans.

Indeed, the aging Anglo population was beginning to feel somewhat smug about its ability to provide for itself. As a generational consciousness took hold after the year 2000, the Baby Boomers' voting rates increased markedly, even beyond what was normally expected for the consistently diligent voters in the 45–65 age category. Realizing that federal benefits were spotty and unreliable, the Baby Boom electorate began to construct state programs to benefit the elderly. Soci-Cal Security was voted in by referendum. Building on the federal Social Security program,

Soci-Cal expanded coverage to include people who had never paid Social Security taxes and people whose private pension plans did not provide comprehensive benefits. Virtually everyone over 65 was to be covered by the program. Benefits were expanded beyond the federal level, to provide complete 65-to-death income-maintenance and medical benefits.

Because of the number of beneficiaries involved, Soci-Cal became the largest single item in the state's budget. Although exact figures were never established, economists estimated that it consumed between 35 percent and 50 percent of the state's annual revenues. Despite occasional grumblings by younger voters about the amount of money Soci-Cal required, the virtually rock-solid voting bloc of people 55 and over made any contraction in coverage an act of political suicide. Indeed, as new needs were discovered, additions were made to the program to cover particular groups or conditions that had not been foreseen by those who drafted the referendum. The voting bloc of elderly was considered a model of generational politics, and political scientists from around the country came to study the organization of an interest group that had brought about the passage of what was now considered to be the national model.

Funding for the Soci-Cal program came both from an expanded state tax base and from cuts in programs that had been targeted for younger groups. After all, the reasoning went, since there were fewer younger people around, there should be less demand for those sorts of services. Among the worst-hit victims were the state's institutions of higher learning. In an effort to keep the funding level for the Soci-Cal program up, several campuses of the University of California system, the state college and university system, and the community college system were closed and auctioned off. The combination of salary savings and capital infusion from the sale of buildings and property to a consortium of offshore businessmen helped balance the state budget for a while.

Meanwhile, trouble had long been brewing on the border. Finally, in 1997, Mexico's ruling party lost its grip on the country. In the space of a few days, overburdened by the nation's foreign debt commitments, some of the top leaders, sensing the failure of the political compromises that had held the country together since 1917, looted the treasuries and bank accounts of the various federal agencies in their charge and fled the country, leaving a bankrupt government. Not only was the foreign debt no longer serviced; the government was simply unable to pay for its own continuation. A succession of military coups followed. Each military government was weaker and shorter-lived than its predecessor. Fearing a recurrence of the revolution that shook Mexico in 1910–17, the wealthy families moved out of the country, shutting down their factories and businesses and leaving caretakers to guard their estates until such time as law and order could be reestablished.

With the Mexican economy at a standstill and the government for all practical purposes nonexistent, the population faced two alternatives: stay in a politically unstable country with no prospects of a restoration of order and no prospects of employment, or move northward to the United States, where there was at least stability. So in a period of 10 years over 10 million Mexicans left the country and followed the route northward that had been blazed by the farmworkers recruited by U.S. agents during the heyday of the bracero program (1943–64). Approximately half, or about five million, found their way to California, another two million went to Texas, and the rest were dispersed across the country.

Technically, of course, these people were not political refugees, and since they had entered illegally, were not eligible to receive any social benefits such as education or health services. At the same time the presence of such a large supply of unskilled but very cheap labor was not lost on astute businessmen, who found in California an ideal climate for the development of assembly plants: political stability, low wages, almost no unionization, and proximity to markets.

To the public at large and specifically the Anglo population, however, this influx of Latinos was an unwelcome development. The passage of strict immigration controls at the federal level after Mexico's collapse had made the non-Latino population feel safe for a while. The implementation of a computerized system for on-the-spot checking of identity cards had also helped to allay people's fears. The qualms of civil libertarians were eased when the decision was made to check the cards of everyone, not just Latin-looking people, at checkpoints that were to be arranged at randomly chosen times and locations. But neither measure stemmed the flow of immigrants. Many agencies, especially those providing social services, instituted their own residency checks. Schools seemed to be a particularly good point for such checks, allowing administrators to screen ineligible children out of the shrinking school system.

Despite all this, the Latino population continued to grow. Most of the petty and violent crime was laid at the door of the Latinos. And even though criminologists pointed out how the ethnic correlation was a function of age, with Latino youths filling most of the slots in the historically high-crime 15–25 bracket, and not a matter of inherent criminality, this argument was lost on an older generation that increasingly began to see itself as the target of ethnically related crime.

Visible police protection was demanded, and when not provided by public entities, privately retained security forces filled the gap. In urban areas the remaining elderly Anglos adopted all sorts of security measures, huddling behind high, tamper-proof fences, with gate guards, canine patrols, entry and exit checks, and thick grills on windows to protect them. Gradually, similar measures were adopted in the suburban residential areas. Though such precautions were not all that necessary in the suburbs, they made the residents feel safe and secure, by keeping the darker, younger population at bay.

And that population persisted in being different. Despite laws mandating the use of English on job sites and in schools, Spanish was still to be heard everywhere on the streets. Many municipalities had passed ordinances outlawing the celebration of any holidays other than "American" holidays, such as the Fourth of July. A measure that puzzled many people outside the state was the declaration passed by local initiative in San Diego County that "American culture" was to be the only culture allowable. There was so much confusion regarding the definition of American culture that the law was considered unenforceable. Nonetheless, the very fact that it was voted in demonstrated that there was much public sentiment to maintain some bulwark against the influence of "non-American" elements.

Between 2000 and 2015 the Anglo population began to feel more comfortable and secure: programs benefiting the Baby Boom generation were growing, and the influence of the Latino population was seemingly being held to a minimum (at least behind the security walls). But pressures were building that would soon threaten the Anglos' tranquility.

Because of the massive funding shifts to the Baby Boom elderly, the younger generation was finding itself increasingly at a disadvantage. To begin with, the school system had deteriorated so badly that by the year 2000 the educational achievement of students had begun to decline. Native-born Latinos were the most severely injured of all groups: each year fewer and fewer of them finished high school or entered into the shrunken university system. Most of the children of the foreign-born Latinos, without benefit of documents, were barred from the classroom, and did not even achieve the primary-school level their parents had attained in Mexico and other parts of Latin America.

The employment patterns of Latinos were weighted toward the areas needing unskilled labor. Because of the massive waves of immigrants, California had become a repository of unskilled labor, and a labor surplus kept wages low. This had encouraged the construction of assembly plants for products developed and partially manufactured elsewhere. Large corporations from both the east coast and the Orient had discovered the advantage of having assembly plants in California rather than in Mexico and other politically or economically unstable countries. Because of the decline in educational and research activities, California had long since ceased to be the center of high technology research and development. Indeed, most of the activities requiring a highly educated work force, such as product design, had shifted away from the state by the mid-1990's. The high cost of land and the high taxes imposed by the state to fund its old-age security programs helped to push the remaining industries out.

No longer a leader in the Pacific Rim economy, California was now content with exporting primary foodstuffs. In fact, so vicious was the downward spiral in the California economy that the state began to look a little like an underdeveloped country—exporting primary products for a relatively cheap price and importing consumer goods for a fairly high price. The only local industry left that was totally in the hands of Californians was light industry, which manufactured some articles for local consumption. The sheer size of the economy was impressive, but sharp-eyed economists and investors had noted the shift in activities at its base, and investment capital no longer flowed from the Pacific Rim into California, except into small projects that could take advantage of the seemingly inexhaustible supply of cheap labor.

Few Anglos were personally touched by this shift in the state's economic base. Because of the overabundance of cheap labor, it had become customary for almost all non-Latinos to have at least one Latino servant. Many of the elderly Baby Boomers were able to hire two or three people to keep house, as well as to provide the care and attention they needed in their old age.

The younger population, a large portion of which was now Latino, felt itself caught in a squeeze. Elderly benefit contributions alone accounted for nearly 40 percent of the payroll taxes. Federal income tax rates were also quite high, to cover both the increasing cost of additional benefits programs for the elderly and the continuing cost of expensive military systems. On top of all this the state income tax took nearly another 20 percent, most of it destined for California's elderly benefits package, Soci-Cal Security. The younger workers saw huge amounts of their paychecks eaten up to fund programs for the elderly with little in the way of benefits returned to them. Never mind the failing school system for their children—capital expenditures for roads, water systems, and public buildings and spaces had dwindled to almost nothing. Not only were old structures falling into disrepair; new services were usually not available in the areas of heaviest Latino population growth. By the turn of the century it had become common to see unpaved roads in the Latino sections of towns and to find hoses and electrical lines snaking along the ground, sometimes for miles, to provide water and electricity in areas where no other form of service was available.

The older, native-born Latinos chafed under the burden, feeling a resentment that their children were not able to enjoy public benefits that the Baby Boomers had enjoyed while they were growing up: free, good education at all levels; public health services such as the old polio vaccine campaigns; paved roads; public parks and lands. A drive into a Latino town after the year 2000 was likened by some to a drive through a typical town in undeveloped parts of Latin America: the dust, the hunger, the throngs of unemployed, the stench of burning garbage, the listless, apathetic, defeated look of people in the streets.

The Californians who had been born in the state between 1970 and 1990 were the most frustrated. Most of their parents were safely in the Baby Boom generation, and from them they had heard of how good the life in the state had once been. Consequently, they had been raised with certain aspirations. But now, however hard they worked, they found themselves quite unable to fulfill those aspirations. Between taxes to support the elderly and the high cost of housing, there seemed to be little money left over to support their families on, let alone to satisfy their own desire for consumer goods.

Although many of these workers had managed to find some marginally secure positions in government or industry, they felt increasingly threatened by the constant contraction of programs and the economy. The only growth area seemed to be in providing services to the elderly.

This generation of workers had grown up before residential and school segregation had become so marked, and thus the Latinos had contacts with their non-Latino peers. A breakaway group from the nearly defunct Democratic Party, composed of Latino and non-Latino post–Baby Boomers, began to meet to see how they might create better opportunities for themselves and their children. Gradually, it became clear to this breakaway group that, as the number of elderly continued to swell, their own situation would become still more precarious. Various economic analysts among them argued persuasively that if the services to the elderly were curtailed sharply, by perhaps as much as 70 percent, that income could be used to rebuild the state's infrastructure and invite the outside investment needed to revive the California economy. Recognizing that such a decision was fraught with political dangers, and that no legislator would dare suggest cuts of this magnitude, given the voting power of the elderly, the group decided only an initiative would do. They also recognized that its passage could be accomplished only by appealing to the younger members of the voting-age population, a group that was nearly 50 percent Latino. This would have the effect of making a racial issue out of a generational one, but they saw no alternative.

The ensuing campaign was a partial success; it succeeded in dividing the electorate along generational lines, but the initiative itself failed. In the aftermath, the older generation vowed not to let its security be so threatened again, and activities that could be perceived as political were sharply curtailed. Social meetings and parties by Latinos were routinely broken up, and under the monolingual laws already in effect, Spanish-language radio, television, newspaper, and book-publishing activities were outlawed.

These harsh measures backfired badly. The younger Latinos responded by calling mass demonstrations; violence broke out at many of them when the frightened older generation tried to halt them. Clandestine presses rolled in the Latino barrios, churning out literature designed to incite the younger generation to rebel, to refuse to pay its taxes or cooperate in any other way. Strikes broke out in assembly plants, security walls were set afire and toppled, the sale of guns, and their price, soared in the elderly areas. The younger Latinos painted the elderly as parasites, who had enjoyed all the benefits of society when those benefits were free and now blithely continued to tax the workers to maintain their style of living, without a thought to the damage it was doing to them. The elderly painted the younger Latinos as parasites, as foreigners who were soaking up benefits that should go to the elderly, as non-Americans who were threatening to dilute American culture, as crime-ridden, disease-ridden, and lawless.

The year following the failure of the initiative saw upheaval after upheaval, charge and countercharge. Then both sides retreated temporarily to their strongholds, the elderly behind their security-patrolled villages, the younger Latinos to their unlit, unpaved barrios. Each side prepared for a last assault on the other, either a physical assault or a political assault that would remove the problem permanently.

Civil revolt was only months away.

Projections and Policy Areas

If we consider policy decisions being made today at the local, state, and national level, the above scenario is not beyond the realm of possibility. Decisions have consequences that range far beyond an officeholder's term, yet their long-range consequences are rarely considered.

The number of elderly is growing rapidly, and they will have needs that society must decide whether or not to provide. If the decision is to provide benefits to the elderly, then the support of the elderly will rest on the ability and the willingness of the younger and, specifically, the Latino workers, to assume that burden of support. This future will and ability will be the product of policy decisions made now and in the near-range (10–20 years) future. In this book we will lay out the forces behind these demographic changes, and provide some projections of both Latino growth and elderly growth. These projections will be laid across different policy areas, to see how the fact of an age-ethnic stratified society might affect those areas. For our modeling purposes, we shall consider the areas of employment and income, education, health, political participation, immigration, and culture. After a brief look at the national implications of Latino population growth, we shall conclude on a much happier, more positive best-case scenario.

Chapter Two

California's Population:
Past, Present, and Future

That the U.S. population is aging has become a well-accepted fact. So much coverage has been given to the issue that a detailed analysis of this phenomenon is not in order here. Rather, in this chapter we shall merely outline the major dynamics as a necessary introduction to the following analysis of the population trends in California.

The Dynamics of Demographic Change

The aging of the U.S. population has its roots in changes in the economy and society over the past century, a period that saw the country turn from a primarily rural, agrarian society into a primarily urban, industrial, and postindustrial society. This demographic transition can be best seen in the graphic form commonly used to express the age structure—an age pyramid. To generate such a pyramid as seen in Figure 2.1, the population is divided by sex, and each sex is grouped into five-year cohorts or age groups. The youngest cohorts, ages 0 through 4, are at the base of the pyramid with males on the left and females on the right, the next youngest cohorts, ages 5 through 9, are above, and so forth.

Preindustrial Society

The shape of the age pyramid for the United States in 1860, shown in Figure 2.1, is typical of preindustrial societies, which tend to have both high birth rates and high death rates. Infant and child mortality is especially high, so that though many children are

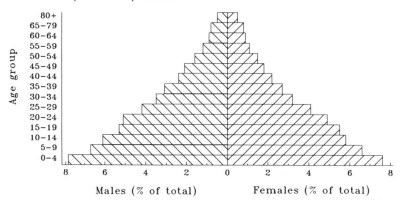

Fig. 2.1. Age structure of the United States, 1860. Source: U.S. Bureau of the Census, *Historical Statistics of the United States, Colonial Times to Present*, part 1 (Washington, D.C., 1976), pp. 119–34.

born in a family, relatively few survive to adulthood. In the age pyramid shown, only 55 of every 100 children born reached the age of 20. Most of these deaths would have been due to childhood diseases, poor nutrition, lack of sanitation, and of course trauma.

Adults in such societies fare only slightly better. Disease, epidemics, trauma, and childbirth complications continue to take their toll, so that there is a constant although slightly lower mortality rate during the reproductive years. Once past their middle years, most adults succumb to the wear and tear of exposure to disease and of years of physical work: death often comes at an age considered quite young by today's standards, with comparatively few people surviving to age 65.

All of this was typical of the preindustrial U.S. society: many people were born, but many died, and the population grew very slowly. Few lived to age 65. This resulted in a fairly young population. The population turnover was quick, and generations were closely spaced.

Industrial Society

As societies become industrialized and urbanized, two important demographic phenomena typically occur: both the death rate and the birth rate fall. Thanks to rising incomes, higher levels of education, and better nutrition and sanitation, the health of the population begins to improve, and the mortality rates drop for all, children, adults, and the elderly. In the United States this drop in mortality began around 1870. The birth rate remained quite high, however, for parents were still not accustomed to the idea that most children would survive to adulthood. Between this higher rate of natural increase and an immigration policy that encouraged massive inflows from other countries, the U.S. population grew rapidly. Then, in about 1910, the U.S. birth rate started to fall (Omran 1977). By 1940 the rates had become quite low, and the U.S. population had achieved its demographic transition from a high fertility, high mortality society to a low fertility, low mortality society.

The age pyramid of a modern industrial society, once it has made such a demographic transition, ceases to resemble a pyramid. Rather than a figure with a wide base and a narrow top (reflecting many births, but also many early deaths), we now find something closer to a rectangle: few children are born, and the vast majority of them survive to old age. The age pyramid for the United States in 1985 (see Fig. 2.2) shows this trend. The different

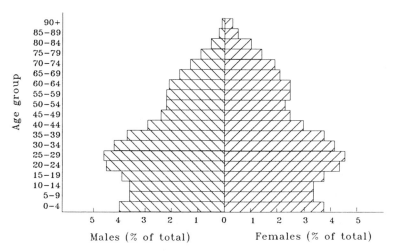

Fig. 2.2. Age structure of the United States, 1985. Source: U.S. Bureau of the Census, *Projections of the Population of the United States by Age, Sex, and Race: 1983 to 2030* (Washington, D.C., 1984), pp. 43–44.

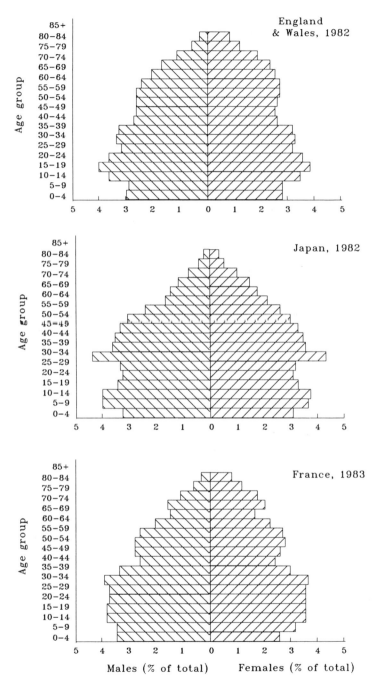

Fig. 2.3. Age structure of England and Wales, Japan, and France, early 1980's. Source: *U.N. Demographic Yearbook, 1985* (New York, 1985), pp. 206–15.

age structures in the United States in 1860 and 1985 reflect the aging of the population. This pattern is common to industrialized societies, as Figure 2.3 shows. But the shape of the U.S. pyramid differs quite markedly from the shape of the pyramids for England and Wales, France, and even Japan. The important difference is the magnitude and duration of the Baby Boom in the United States.

The Baby Boom Anomaly

As we have seen, U.S. birth and death rates were both low by 1940. After the Second World War, the U.S. population experienced a phenomenon that appears to have been unique and short-lived: from 1946 to about 1963 the birth rate showed a marked upswing. The rate then suddenly and rapidly declined, to return to the low level of 1940. This spurt of births, followed by a fall to extremely low fertility patterns, has produced a demographic anomaly. The U.S. "rectangle" has a perceptible bulge. As the population ages, this lump of Baby Boom cohorts will move up the demographic pyramid, creating dislocations by placing demands on age-specific activities, then moving on, leaving in its wake an overabundance of expensive programs, facilities, and policies for the much smaller cohort that replaces it. This process may be appreciated in almost any community school system, where the facilities erected for the Baby Boom generation lie vacant, rooms closed off and windows boarded up, because the Baby Bust generation is too small to fill them. Thirty years ago the building of school facilities was an important policy issue; in the 1980's the proper disposal of those now-excess facilities has become an issue.

As the Baby Boom generation works its way up the demographic pyramid, the swelling and then shrinking of certain age groups produces a shape that some demographers have likened to a python swallowing a pig. Figure 2.4 presents demographic pyramids for the years 2000, 2015, and 2030 based on national population projections by the U.S. Bureau of the Census. The aptness of the python analogy can be appreciated as this generation ages.

The number of elderly will be even further inflated because life expectancy is still increasing gradually. So the Baby Boomers will

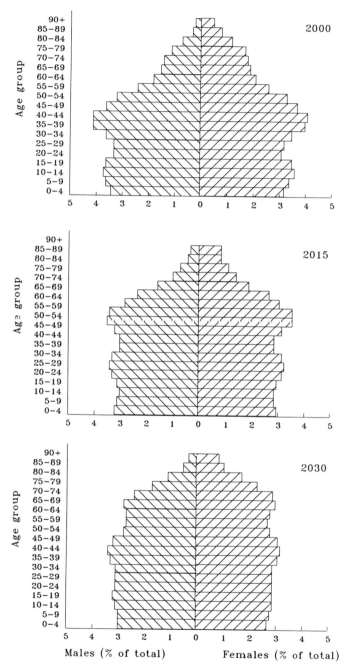

Fig. 2.4. Age structure of the United States, 2000, 2015, and 2030. Source: Same as Fig. 2.2, pp. 73–74, 79–80, 85–88.

not only arrive at age 65 in very large numbers, they may be expected to live for quite some time beyond that age. As was hinted in Chapter 1, the expected result will be a doubling in the percentage of elderly over the period 1985–2020. By 2020 fully 22 percent of the U.S. population will be age 65 and over.

Another way to consider the effect of the aging of the Baby Boom generation is to look at the expected rise in the median age of the U.S. population. In 1985 the median age was 31.8 years and climbing. By 2030 it could be as high as 43.9 years. As a graphic illustration of the dimensions of the demographic changes, past and future, in the United States, we might note that as recently as 1900 *life expectancy* itself was barely 47 years (Omran 1977: 19).

Latino Population Growth

Another dynamic affecting the composition of the state's population is the growth of the Latino population. In 1940, barely 5.6 percent of the population was Latino (EDD 1986: Table 1). By 1980, it had grown to 19.2 percent (USBC 1983b). Fueled by high fertility and immigration, the Latino population appears to be a major component of the population in the future.

Looking at these two trends, the aging of the population and the growth of the Latino population, we wondered if there might be some policy connection between them. In order to determine how these trends will shape California's demographic future, we constructed computer-generated population simulations to create different population scenarios based on varying assumptions.

Population Projections Model

Our population projections model consists of a set of computer programs that calculates the future projected population of California for alternative sets of fertility, mortality, and immigration rates. Since these rates vary greatly for different age, sex, and ethnic groups, we determined the current or recent values of these rates for each five-year age cohort for each sex of each ethnic group. Using California's estimated 1985 population distribution as a starting point,* the computer program calculated the pro-

*See the Appendix for the 1985 population estimation procedure.

jected population distributions implied by each set of assumptions. The set of assumptions that we believe to be most likely or plausible resulted in our *baseline* population projection. We also calculated a number of alternative projections meant to illustrate the effects of different combinations of fertility, mortality, and migration trends on future population composition. We believe that some of these alternative simulations or scenarios are quite implausible. But they serve to illustrate the importance of different factors on future population distributions. For example, one of our projections is calculated on the basis of the complete cessation of migration from Latin America. While we believe that this is very unlikely, this projection serves to show that the Latino population will grow rapidly even if there were no migration.

In Figure 2.5 we present the age pyramid for California for 1985, with its telltale Baby Boom bulge. The three factors that operate together to change the shape of the pyramid—mortality, migration, and fertility—are shown as forces acting on the pyramid.

In projecting population growth in California, the three components of change are fertility as expressed in live births to women

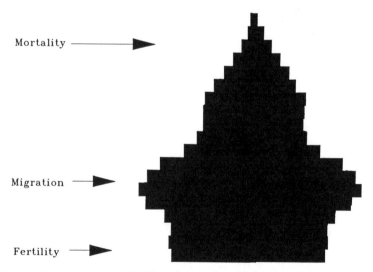

Fig. 2.5. Age structure of California in 1985 and the forces that shaped it

of childbearing age, mortality as reflected in cohort survival rates, and estimated net migration, the difference between people moving into the state and those leaving. All projections developed for this work are based on the state's estimated baseline population for 1985. Individual cohorts are determined by sex (male and female), by age (five-year intervals from 0–4 years through 85–89 years, with a residual 90 years and older group), and by ethnicity (Anglos, Blacks, Asians, and Latinos, the last split into native-born and foreign-born groups). The rationale for disaggregating the population into this many groups is that fertility, mortality, and migration differ for the various cohorts; furthermore, as considered in subsequent scenarios, labor force participation and income levels differ for various groups.

Data used to calibrate the various models come from three categories: first, cross-sectional data, such as from the 1980 Census Public Use Microdata Sample (PUMS), which provide highly detailed information on California age-specific and ethnic-specific fertility rates and the like; second, published analyses of registered deaths by age, sex, and ethnicity; and third, time-series data, such as from the U.S. Census Bureau's series of Current Population Survey (CPS) reports, which provide information on how the model parameters change over time, though often with little detail and with problems inherent in changing definitions and coverage.

Fertility

Fertility rates changed substantially over the 40 years between 1940 and 1980. Table 2.1 shows the crude birth rate in California from 1940 to 1980. As may be seen, fertility jumped between 1945 and 1947, with the period of high fertility continuing into the early 1960's. This is the well-documented "Baby Boom."

Replacement fertility, that level at which one generation will replace itself if all other factors remain constant, is approximately 2.1 children per woman (Pressat 1985: 200). As illustrated in Figure 2.6, in California only the foreign-born Latinos had a fertility rate above the replacement rates and Anglos, Blacks, and Asians were all substantially below it. The total completed fertility for Latinas in 1980 was 2.5, compared with 1.31 for Anglos, 1.59 for

TABLE 2.1
Crude Birth Rates, California, 1940–1980
(Births per 1,000 population)

Year	CBR	Year	CBR	Year	CBR
1940	16.2	1954	24.4	1968	17.5
1941	17.3	1955	24.1	1969	17.9
1942	19.8	1956	24.6	1970	18.1
1943	20.4	1957	24.7	1971	16.2
1944	19.8	1958	23.7	1972	14.9
1945	19.5	1959	23.5	1973	14.3
1946	22.7	1960	23.7	1974	14.7
1947	24.8	1961	23.2	1975	14.7
1948	23.8	1962	22.3	1976	15.1
1949	23.7	1963	21.7	1977	15.5
1950	23.1	1964	20.8	1978	15.6
1951	23.4	1965	19.2	1979	16.3
1952	24.2	1966	17.9	1980	16.9
1953	24.5	1967	17.6		

SOURCE: California Department of Health Services, Center for Health Statistics, *Vital Statistics of California, 1979–80* (Sacramento, 1980), p. 17.

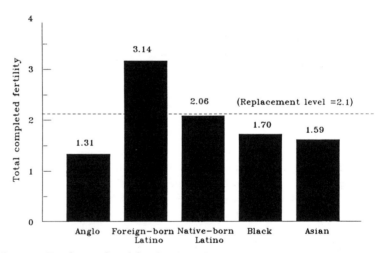

Fig. 2.6. Total completed fertility by ethnicity, California, 1980. Source: U.S. Bureau of the Census, *Census of Population and Housing, 1980: Public Use Microdata Sample A, California* (Washington, D.C., 1983).

Asians and others, and 1.70 for Blacks. If the foreign-born Latinas are singled out, the figure climbs to 3.14, compared with 2.06 for the U.S.-born. Although the fertility rate among the U.S.-born Latinas is, like that of the general population, below replacement level, it is still substantially higher than the rate for all other groups.

The population projections of this study reflect two alternative sets of assumptions relating to fertility. The baseline assumption is that the fertility of Anglos, Blacks, and Asians will remain unchanged from the above levels, that the U.S.-born Latinos' fertility rate will decline to the Blacks' 1980 level by the year 2030, and that the foreign-born Latino fertility rates will proportionately decline to the U.S.-born Latinos' 1980 level by 2030. The second assumption, which we call the Rapid Fertility Decline Alternative, is that the fertility rates of all minority groups will decline to the 1980 Anglo rate by the year 2000 and will remain at that level to 2030. Although fertility has risen among some cohorts since 1980, particularly Anglos in the 30-to-39 age group, this "Baby Boomlet" was not incorporated into our fertility assumptions: it appears to be the temporary result of a catch-up on delayed families by the aging Baby Boomers, and the comparatively minor change involved would, in any case, not markedly change the projection results.

Mortality

Life expectancy at birth differs significantly for men and women and for various ethnic groups. This is illustrated in Table 2.2, which shows that there is a gap of 20.2 years between Asian women, who have the highest life expectancy, 85.8 years, and Black men, who have the lowest, 65.6 years. Estimates of mortality by age, sex, and ethnicity for the projection model of this study were drawn from "California Life Expectancy: Abridged Life Tables" (CDHS 1983a), which provides detailed mortality and survival statistics by five-year age cohorts, race, and sex.

Advances in public health and medicine, alterations in working conditions and environment, and changes in lifestyle are among the many factors that have resulted in sharp increases in life expectancy during the twentieth century. In 1930 the life expectancy

TABLE 2.2
Life Expectancy at Birth by Sex and Ethnicity,
California, 1979–1981

Sex	Anglo	Black	Asian	Latino	Total
Both sexes	*74.9*	*69.9*	*82.5*	*75.5*	*74.8*
Males	71.3	65.6	79.2	72.0	71.3
Females	78.4	74.3	85.8	79.4	78.3

SOURCE: California Department of Health Services, Center for Health Statistics, *Data Matters* (Sacramento, July 1983), pp. 16–17.
NOTE: Latino defined as Spanish surname.

of California Anglo males at birth was 58.6 years and 63.7 for Anglo females. By 1980, as we see in Table 2.2, Anglo males in California had a life expectancy of 71.3 years, a gain of 12.7 years. The life expectancy of Anglo women had risen even more sharply, to 78.4 years, a gain of 14.7 years in 50 years. A significant part of these gains was made in the 1970's. For all races and sexes life expectancy rose 3.1 years between 1970 and 1980, from 71.7 years to 74.8 years (CDHS 1983a).

Based on these trends, our baseline projections assume a 5-year increase in life expectancy for all groups between 1985 and 2030. Alternative simulations were run assuming no increase and a 10-year increase by 2030. For comparison, a 3.5-year increase is projected in California Department of Finance (1981); and the U.S. Bureau of the Census (1984) projects an increase of 2.4 years between 1982 (74.3 years) and 2000 (76.7 years) with an additional 4.3-year increase in the 80-year period to 2080.

Underestimating increases in life expectancy would cause underestimates in the burden of intergenerational support, and conversely for overestimates. Although recent gains in life expectancy may be more difficult to maintain in the future, raising the life expectancy of all races to the levels currently achieved by Asians living in California would result in an increase midway between our baseline and 10-year simulations.

Immigration

California has been a land of migrants for many years. In each decennial census between 1940 and 1980 over half the residents reported they were born out of state. Table 2.3 shows that the 1980 figure of 45.7 percent of California-born residents was the highest proportion in 40 years. Of the remaining 54.3 percent in that year, more than a third were born in the United States; since then there has been a greater trend toward foreign immigration. Anglo and Black populations have been becoming increasingly California-born, and the Latino and Asian populations more foreign-born. Between 1970 and 1980 alone, foreign-born Latinos jumped from 24.7 percent of all Latinos to 37.0 percent, and foreign-born Asians surged from 36.4 percent to 50.2 percent.

A Baseline Projection

There are countless ways of combining alternative fertility, mortality, and net immigration assumptions in a study like ours.

TABLE 2.3
Population by Ethnicity and Place of Birth, California, 1940–1980
(Population in thousands)

Category	1940	1950	1960	1970	1980
Total population	6,677	11,852	15,735	19,924	23,713
California-born (%)	36.3	42.4	39.9	43.1	45.7
Other U.S.-born (%)	49.1	48.6	51.6	47.0	39.1
Foreign-born (%)	14.6	9.1	8.5	9.9	15.2
Anglo total	6,001	9,980	13,045	15,733	16,206
California-born (%)	35.1	41.1	38.6	42.1	46.6
Other U.S.-born (%)	51.7	50.9	54.3	50.5	46.0
Foreign-born (%)	13.2	8.0	7.1	7.5	7.4
Black total	131	594	867	1,394	1,819
California-born (%)	22.8	25.7	31.7	39.5	43.4
Other U.S.-born (%)	74.5	73.7	67.5	58.9	54.1
Foreign-born (%)	2.7	0.6	0.7	1.6	2.5
Asian total	171	269	385	658	1,855
California-born (%)	54.3	59.7	47.7	41.8	34.5
Other U.S.-born (%)	5.8	9.8	21.4	21.8	15.3
Foreign-born (%)	39.9	30.5	30.9	36.4	50.2
Latino total	374	1,009	1,457	2,139	3,833
California-born (%)	52.6	59.8	55.0	53.4	48.7
Other U.S.-born (%)	17.5	21.4	25.6	21.9	14.3
Foreign-born (%)	29.9	18.8	19.4	24.7	37.0

SOURCE: California Employment Development Department, *Socio-Economic Trends in California, 1940–1980* (Sacramento, 1986), pp. 10–11.
NOTE: Latino defined as Spanish surname.

The combination we chose for our baseline simulation was (1) fertility change as outlined above (unchanged in 2030 from the 1980 level for Anglos, Blacks, and Asians; slow decline to the Blacks' 1980 level for U.S.-born Latinas; slow decline to the U.S.-born Latinas' 1980 level for foreign-born Latinas); (2) a five-year increase in life expectancy by 2030; and (3) a constant net immigration of 250,000 people a year of which 100,000 will be Latinos. Six other combinations were investigated (see Table 2.4).

Our baseline projection results are that California's population will grow at a decreasing rate (Table 2.5). From 1985 to the year 2000, the population is projected to increase from 26.2 million to 32.2 million, for an increase of 6.0 million, or 23 percent, over the 15-year period. From 2000 to 2015, the increase is projected to be 5.2 million for 16 percent growth, and in the next 15 years to 2030, the change is 4.2 million for 11 percent. This comparatively smooth deceleration in growth masks a radical underlying change. Of the 15.4-million-person growth between 1985 and 2030, Latino growth would account for 60 percent, while the growth of the

TABLE 2.4
Assumptions for California Population Projections, 1985–2030

Simulation	Fertility	Life expectancy[a]	Net annual immigration[b]
Baseline	—[c]	+5 years	250,000
No foreign immigration (floor figure)	—[c]	+5 years	95,000
Latino influx (ceiling figure)	—[c]	+5 years	650,000
High life expectancy	—[c]	+10 years	250,000
Low life expectancy	—[c]	No gain	250,000
Rapid fertility decline	All at Anglo 1985 by 2000	+5 years	250,000
No Latino immigration	—[c]	+5 years	150,000

[a]Gain by 2030 from 1980 level.
[b]This figure represents migration into California from other states as well as international migration. It is constant at 250,000 people per year (of whom 100,000 are Latinos) except for the "No foreign immigration," "Latino-influx," and "No Latino immigration" scenarios.
[c]Between 1980 and 2030 Anglo, Black, and Asian fertility rates are held constant at their current level. It is further assumed that by 2030 U.S.-born Latino fertility gradually decreases to 1980 Black level (1.7) and that foreign-born Latino rates decrease to 1980 U.S.-born Latino level (2.1).

TABLE 2.5
Population Projections by Age and Ethnicity, California, 1985–2030, Baseline Assumptions
(Population in millions)

Category	1985	2000	2015	2030
Total	*26.22*	*32.24*	*37.39*	*41.58*
Youth	5.86	6.24	6.32	6.34
Working age	17.48	21.94	25.37	25.94
Elderly	2.88	4.06	5.70	9.29
Anglo	16.77	17.94	18.26	17.98
Black	2.04	2.63	3.17	3.64
Asian	1.83	2.98	4.12	5.19
Latino	5.58	8.68	11.84	14.76
Anglo				
Youth	3.02	2.65	2.25	1.97
Working age	11.36	12.26	12.24	10.59
Elderly	2.39	3.04	3.78	5.43
Black				
Youth	0.55	0.61	0.65	0.68
Working age	1.36	1.80	2.17	2.33
Elderly	0.13	0.22	0.34	0.62
Asian				
Youth	0.44	0.59	0.72	0.83
Working age	1.26	2.07	2.75	3.22
Elderly	0.13	0.32	0.66	1.15
Latino				
Youth	1.85	2.39	2.71	2.87
Working age	3.51	5.82	8.20	9.80
Elderly	0.22	0.48	0.92	2.09

NOTE: Youth is defined as 0–15 years, working age as 16–64 years, and elderly as 65 and over in this and subsequent tables. Columns may not sum because of rounding.

Anglo population would account for only 8 percent. For the period 2015 to 2030, the Anglo population declines by over 250,000. The number of youths aged 0 to 15 years remains essentially unchanged over the entire baseline projection, rising only 8 percent in 45 years. By contrast, the working-age population (ages 16–64) grows by 26 percent between 1985 and 2000, grows an additional 15.6 percent in the next 15 years (to 2015), and then nearly ceases to grow, changing by only 570,000 or 2.2 percent, over the 15 years to 2030. The senior cohort aged 65 years and older jumps dramatically; by 41 percent between 1985 and 2000,

26   *California's Population*

TABLE 2.6
Population by Ethnicity, California, 1940–1980

Year	Anglo	Black	Asian	Latino	Total
1940					
Millions	6.01	0.13	0.17	0.37	6.69
Percent	89.90	2.00	2.60	5.60	100.00%
1950					
Millions	10.04	0.60	0.27	1.01	11.92
Percent	84.20	5.00	2.30	8.50	100.00%
1960					
Millions	13.05	0.87	0.39	1.46	15.75
Percent	82.80	5.50	2.40	9.30	100.00%
1970					
Millions	15.73	1.39	0.66	2.14	19.92
Percent	79.00	7.00	3.30	10.70	100.00%
1980					
Millions	16.21	1.82	1.85	3.83	23.71
Percent	68.30	7.70	7.80	16.20	100.00%
1980					
Millions	15.91	1.80	1.44	4.57	23.71
Percent	67.07	7.60	6.06	19.26	100.00%

SOURCE: Same as Table 2.3, p. 9.
NOTE: Latino defined as Spanish surname except for the second set of 1980 figures, which are based on census self-identified Hispanics.

by another 40 percent in the next 15 years, and finally by 63 percent in the period 2015 to 2030. These data, as well as breakdowns by age with race, are shown in Table 2.5.

The historical relative decline of the Anglo population in California is revealed in Table 2.6, which shows the downward trend from 89.9 percent of the population in 1940 to slightly over two-thirds in 1980. Table 2.7 shows that by 2030, under baseline assumptions, Anglos will constitute only 43 percent of the population. Short of immediate extremely restrictive changes in immigration practice, the Anglo population will be a minority sometime around the turn of the century. One of our simulations examines the possibility of a sharp influx of Latinos at the end of the twentieth century. Although we have not examined the implications, clearly there is the potential for large influxes from Asia. The likelihood of no foreign immigration between now and 2030 is essentially zero. Thus our no-immigration simulation is an absolute lower bound.

As may be seen in Table 2.8, a transformation of the age structure of the California population occurred during the 1940's, when
fertility rates rose dramatically, causing the percentage of young
people aged 0–15 to jump from 21.8 percent to 34.2 percent; at
the same time the number of working-age adults dropped from
70.3 percent to 60.2 percent; finally, seniors aged 65 or older declined from 7.9 percent to 5.6 percent. As discussed above, fertility remained high during the 1950's and dropped in the early
1960's. Thus, the "Baby Boom," which began in the 1940's, can be

TABLE 2.7
Population by Ethnicity, California, 2030, on Different Assumptions

Category	Anglo	Black	Asian	Latino	Total
1985 population					
Millions	16.77	2.04	1.83	5.58	26.22
Percent	63.97	7.77	6.99	21.28	100.00%
Baseline 2030					
Millions	17.98	3.64	5.19	14.76	41.58
Percent	43.25	8.75	12.49	35.51	100.00%
No foreign immigration (floor)					
Millions	17.98	3.64	2.17	8.87	32.63
Percent	55.06	11.13	6.64	27.17	100.00%
Latino influx (ceiling)					
Millions	17.98	3.64	5.19	22.27	49.08
Percent	36.64	7.41	10.38	45.37	100.00%
High life expectancy					
Millions	18.89	3.79	5.30	15.11	43.09
Percent	43.84	8.80	12.29	35.06	100.00%
Low life expectancy					
Millions	16.99	3.46	5.07	14.37	39.89
Percent	42.58	8.68	12.72	36.02	100.00%
Low fertility					
Millions	17.98	3.20	4.86	11.80	37.84
Percent	47.53	8.45	12.83	31.19	100.00%
No Latino immigration					
Millions	17.98	3.64	5.19	8.87	35.69
Percent	50.39	10.19	14.55	24.87	100.00%

28   *California's Population*

TABLE 2.8
Population by Age Group, California, 1940–1980

Year	Youth	Working age	Elderly	Total
1940				
Millions	1.45	4.70	0.53	6.69
Percent	21.80	70.30	7.90	100.00%
1950				
Millions	4.08	7.17	0.67	11.92
Percent	34.20	60.20	5.60	100.00%
1960				
Millions	5.03	9.38	1.34	15.75
Percent	31.90	59.60	8.50	100.00%
1970				
Millions	5.95	12.17	1.80	19.92
Percent	29.90	61.60	9.10	100.00%
1980				
Millions	5.64	15.66	2.40	23.71
Percent	23.80	66.10	10.10	100.00%

SOURCE: Same as Table 2.3, pp. 13–15.

seen to have ended in the 1960's. Fertility rates continued to decline, resulting in the "Baby Bust"; this is shown by the drop of the Youth cohort share to 23.8 percent in 1980.

This aging of the Baby Boom generation is one of the most consequential trends of our age, and as shown in Table 2.9, translates into a substantially larger elderly population by 2030 under any reasonable set of assumptions. The issue, as with the growth of the minority population, is not "if," but "how much?" For the year 2030, our baseline projection is for 22.4 percent of the population to be 65 or older; the range of percentages across all of our simulations is from a low of 19.2 percent in the Latino influx scenario to a high of 26.4 percent under the condition of no foreign migration. By all measures, the burden of support of the elderly will increase greatly over current levels.

Conclusions

The various projections for growth to the year 2030 of the Latino population (Table 2.7) combine three possible scenarios ranging from a low floor of 24.9 percent (assuming no Latino immigra-

TABLE 2.9
Population by Age, California, 2030, on Different Assumptions

Category	Youth	Working age	Elderly	Total
1985 population				
Millions	5.86	17.48	2.88	26.22
Percent	22.33	66.68	10.99	100.00%
Baseline 2030				
Millions	6.34	25.94	9.29	41.58
Percent	15.26	62.39	22.35	100.00%
No foreign immigration (floor)				
Millions	4.48	19.55	8.63	32.63
Percent	13.73	59.85	26.42	100.00%
Latino influx (ceiling)				
Millions	7.81	31.10	10.16	49.08
Percent	16.52	64.26	19.22	100.00%
High life expectancy				
Millions	6.36	26.23	10.50	43.09
Percent	14.76	60.88	24.36	100.00%
Low life expectancy				
Millions	6.32	25.58	7.99	39.89
Percent	15.85	64.12	20.03	100.00%
Low fertility				
Millions	4.62	23.92	9.29	37.84
Percent	12.22	63.22	24.56	100.00%
No Latino immigration				
Millions	5.03	21.60	9.06	35.69
Percent	14.10	60.15	25.39	100.00%

tion—nearly impossible) to a ceiling of 45.4 percent (assuming a major Latino influx—perhaps all too likely, unfortunately for Mexico). Our baseline model projects a slow, steady growth, with Latinos constituting 35.5 percent of the state's population by the year 2030. This figure should be taken as a reasonable working figure, keeping in mind that political and economic instability in Mexico and Central America may easily produce a sudden, sharp increase in immigration from those areas at any time.

No matter how we change the assumptions in the model, all indications point to a large growth in the Latino population. Under the baseline assumptions it will more than double by 2030, and under increasingly likely assumptions it will grow fivefold.

So, demographically, there are only two questions: not will the Latino population grow substantially, but when will it grow and at what rate?

And on the policy level, the most important question then becomes: What does this growth imply for a state whose overall population is gradually becoming older?

Chapter Three

The Age-Ethnic Gap

Here we examine in greater detail the two major demographic processes at work in the California population: the aging of the Baby Boomers, which will lead to a more than tripling of the 65-and-over population by the year 2030, and the growth of the Latinos, which will lead to a near tripling of their numbers by that time. These two processes might not be so remarkable in themselves were it not for one important fact: the age structures of the Latino and non-Latino populations are very different. The non-Latino population is old and becoming older; the Latino population is young and will remain so in comparison to the rest of the population. In many respects, the two populations may be said to inhabit different generations. The policy significance of these different generational positions will be examined in this chapter.

Portents of Ethnic and Generational Collision

Since immigration from Mexico is a key element in the growth of California's Latino population, it is instructive to consider how sharply the one locale differs from the other in its age structure. Figure 3.1 gives the age pyramids for both Mexico and California as of 1980. Looking first at the Mexican pyramid, we see the classic shape of a not yet fully industrialized society in which many children are born and many die. Moreover, the mortality rate is fairly high in all age cohorts, so that relatively few of those who survive to adulthood reach age 65. The median age in 1978 was 17 years. California's pyramid shows the typical age structure of an industrial or postindustrial society. Its more or less rectangular

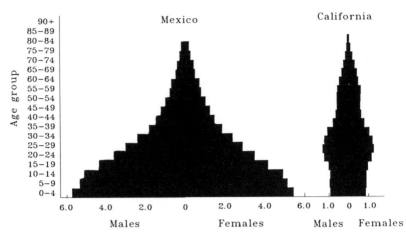

Fig. 3.1. Age structure of Mexico and California, 1980. In these population pyramids and the others in this chapter, population is in millions. Source: *Mexico*, Consejo Nacional de Poblacion, *Mexico: Estimaciones y Proyecciones de Poblacion, 1950–2000* (Mexico, D.F., 1982), p. 44.

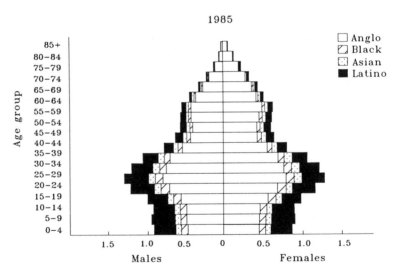

Fig. 3.2. Age structure by ethnicity, California, 1985

shape indicates that relatively few children are born and most survive to live to a fairly advanced age. The median age of the state's Anglo population in 1980 was 34.3 years. There is nearly a whole generation's difference between the two medians.

This disparity is what caught our attention. Appreciating that the state's burgeoning Latino population, nearly 20 percent of the total and growing fast, consists almost entirely of people of Mexican origin, people who are likely therefore to be much younger on the whole than the non-Latino population, we asked ourselves what would happen if the Latino population continued to grow at this same rate as the non-Latino population aged. A glance at the age pyramids alone suggested that a certain stratification by age and ethnicity would almost certainly occur in a very short while. In other words, it seemed likely that in the not-too-distant future, California would become a state of elderly Anglos and young Latinos.

In Figure 3.2 the 1985 age pyramid for the state of California is broken down by ethnic group. We note that in the two youngest cohorts (ages 0–4 and 5–9) approximately half of the children are Latinos or other minorities, and that as one moves up into the older groups, the Latino and minority representation increasingly diminishes, until, at age 65, it can hardly be discerned; almost all the population is Anglo.

Using the baseline assumptions for fertility, mortality, and immigration set out in Chapter 2 (slowly declining fertility, five-year longevity increase, and 100,000 Latinos out of a total of 250,000 immigrants annually), we have "aged" this pyramid to see what the population might look like in the years 2000, 2015, and 2030. The results are shown in Figures 3.3–3.5.

A couple of trends are noticed immediately. The first is that the Baby Boom bulges its way upward, until, in the year 2015, its earliest cohort has fully passed into the retirement age of 65. At that point the young, working-age population becomes increasingly composed of Latinos and other minorities. This trend continues in the years to 2030, with the 65-and-over group becoming larger as more and more of the Baby Boomers join it, and the younger, working-age adult population becoming more and more Latino and other minority.

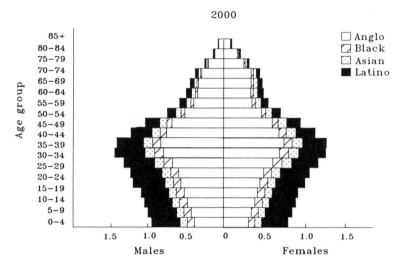

Fig. 3.3. Age structure by ethnicity, California, 2000, baseline assumptions

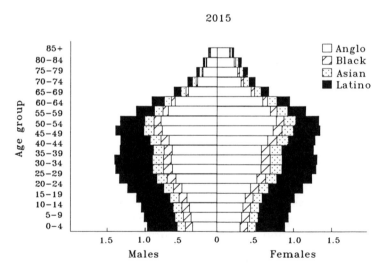

Fig. 3.4. Age structure by ethnicity, California, 2015, baseline assumptions

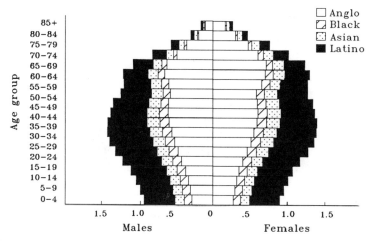

2030

Age group

85+
80-84
75-79
70-74
65-69
60-64
55-59
50-54
45-49
40-44
35-39
30-34
25-29
20-24
15-19
10-14
5-9
0-4

☐ Anglo
▨ Black
⊡ Asian
■ Latino

1.5   1.0   .5   0   .5   1.0   1.5

Males   Females

Fig. 3.5. Age structure by ethnicity, California, 2030, baseline assumptions

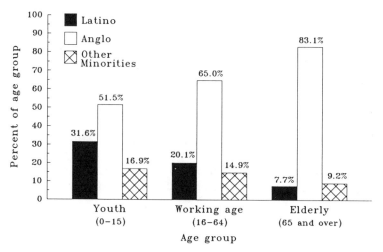

Fig. 3.6. Ethnic composition of major age groups, California, 1985

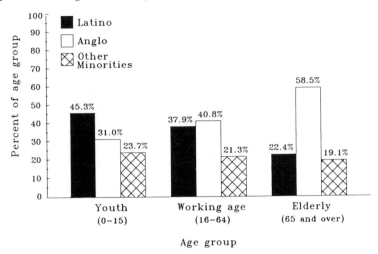

Fig. 3.7. Ethnic composition of major age groups, California, 2030, baseline assumptions

The two major non-Latino ethnic groups in the state (Blacks and Asians) tend to follow the "normal" age structure pattern; that is, they tend to be roughly equally represented in all age groups. The increasingly large contingent of Latinos, however, will be distributed unequally in the different generations. This trend was already seen in 1985, when Latinos were 32 percent of the youth (ages 0–15), 20 percent of those in the working age group (16–64), and less than 8 percent of the elderly. In all generations, Anglos were the majority population (see Fig. 3.6). But the imbalance will be much more severe in 2030: Latinos will then account for fully 45 percent of the youth, and almost 38 percent of the working-age group. Their proportion of the elderly will have risen to 22 percent, but well over half of all the elderly will still be Anglo (see Fig. 3.7).

Latino Growth—Different Scenarios

In percentage and absolute numbers, the Latinos are the most rapidly growing population in California. This growth is due largely to two demographic phenomena: high fertility and immigration. Any change in the fertility and any change in the level of immigration will affect the rate of Latino population growth. Let us vary the assumptions about these two factors, and about mortality, to see how they change this growth. In Figure 3.8 we have summarized Latino growth figures for different immigration assumptions.

Baseline Assumptions

Five-year longevity increase, slow fertility decline, constant immigration. If fertility declined slowly as described under the baseline assumption, Latino immigration remained constant at 100,000 per year, and longevity increased by five years for all, the Latino population would reach 14.8 million by 2030, an increase of 9.2 million over the 1985 figure. At that level, the Latino population would constitute 35.5 percent of the population.

Floor and Ceiling Assumptions

Floor assumptions: No foreign immigration, slow fertility decline, five-year longevity increase. If Latino fertility dropped per our baseline assumptions by 2030, if the longevity of the general population increased by five years by 2030, and if all foreign immigration

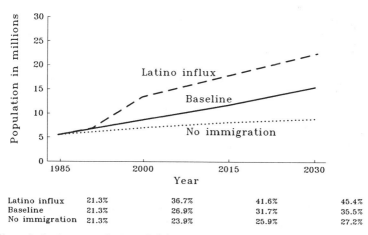

	1985	2000	2015	2030
Latino influx	21.3%	36.7%	41.6%	45.4%
Baseline	21.3%	26.9%	31.7%	35.5%
No immigration	21.3%	23.9%	25.9%	27.2%

Fig. 3.8. Latino population, California, 1985–2030, on different immigration assumptions

ceased in 1985, the Latino population would still grow to 8.9 million. This would represent an increase of 57 percent over the 1985 figure, and Latinos would be 27 percent of the population. This low growth is unlikely, since substantial immigration appears certain to continue into the future. It is important to notice effects on the age structure. In Figure 3.9 we can see, quite literally, the top-heavy demographic pyramid, with a large number of elderly overwhelming the decreasing number of working-age people.

Ceiling assumptions: Immigration influx. If the no-immigration assumption presents an impossibly low "floor" figure, a different assumption may be used to set a "ceiling" figure. The annual number of Mexican immigrants has varied greatly during the twentieth century. In the early years of the twentieth century, there was a governmental collapse in Mexico, followed by a revolution that bordered on fratricidal civil war. During the period from 1911 to 1917, about 10 percent of the population emigrated to the United States; about half of these people found their way to California (Sanchez-Albornoz 1974: 225; Colegio de Mexico 1970: 6). This proportion holds today: about half of all emigrants from Mexico head for California.

It is not beyond the realm of possibility that Mexico could experience another political-economic tragedy on the same scale. The country's current economic problems, exacerbated by a potential political instability, could quite conceivably lead to a national collapse much like the earlier one. We cannot discount such a happening. Indeed, given the impact of the previous sudden infusion of immigrants on the size and age composition of the U.S. Latino population, it would be prudent to get at least some idea of what the recurrence of a Latino immigration influx could portend. Under our model, let us assume a political collapse in Mexico in the year 1990, followed by economic and social disorder. If the revolution of 1910–17 is any pattern, we might then expect about 10 percent of the population of Mexico to emigrate, with about half of the emigrants settling in California.

Let us examine the effect of such a surge in California. First, we assume that the Latino population will be growing by the baseline model assumptions. Then, we add to this the assumption that about 5 percent of the population of Mexico in 1990 would settle

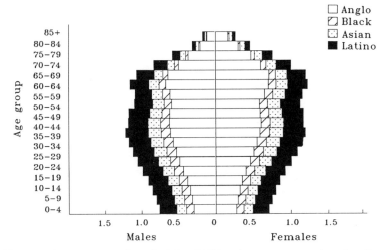

Fig. 3.9. Age structure by ethnicity, California, 2030, on no-immigration assumption

within 10 years in California. The effect would be a sharp increase in Latino population of 500,000 per year for 10 years, from 1990 to 1999. We then assume that immigration would settle back to the regularly projected 100,000 per year, as the political and economic situation in Mexico gradually stitches itself together, as it did once before in this century. Such a sudden influx would have a long-lasting impact. The Latino population would increase dramatically from 1990 to 2000, with the addition of 13.6 million people, above and beyond the baseline figure, by the turn of the century. By the year 2030 the Latino population would jump to 22.3 million, and represent over 45 percent of the state's population.

Figure 3.10 shows what the age pyramid would then look like in the year 2030. The general trend is clearly the same: Latinos would occupy the younger cohorts, and Anglos would dominate the oldest ones. But now there is an even greater proportion of Latinos in the younger cohorts than under the baseline assumption: they become 55.5 percent of all youth and 48.1 percent of all working-age adults. But they are still a distinct minority of the elderly—29.1 percent. Thus, although an immigration surge would result in a substantial increase in the young and working-

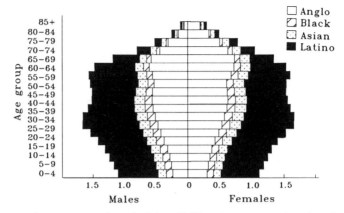

Fig. 3.10. Age structure by ethnicity, California, 2030, on immigration-influx assumption

age Latino populations, the numbers of Latino elderly would be little affected. A majority of the elderly would in fact still be Anglo (53.5 percent), but the Anglo share of the working-age population would fall from 40.8 percent under the baseline assumptions to 34.0 percent.

As will be seen in Chapter 4, this kind of sudden surge is neither as farfetched as one might think nor as threatening. Clearly the party to be most harmed would be Mexico itself, with so massive a loss of working population.

Other Assumptions

Rapid fertility decline, constant immigration, five-year longevity increase. If Latino (as well as Black and Asian) fertility dropped rapidly, so that it equaled Anglo fertility by 2000, assuming constant immigration of 100,000 Latinos per year and a five-year longevity increase, the Latino population would reach 11.8 million by 2030, 31.2 percent of the total population. Fertility is unlikely to drop this rapidly.

Ten-year longevity increase, slow fertility decline, and constant immigration. A 10-year increase in longevity of the entire population, with slow fertility decline and constant immigration, would have the effect of slightly increasing the number of Latinos to 15.1 million by the year 2030. This slight increase, however, would be more than overshadowed by the increase in the number of elderly overall, so that Latinos would actually constitute a slightly smaller proportion of the total population than with only a five-year longevity increase: 35.1 percent.

No longevity increase, slow fertility decline, constant immigration. A converse phenomenon is seen if there were to be no increase in longevity. The absolute number of Latinos would drop to 14.4 million, but their representation would climb by about one-half of 1 percent, to a 36.0 percent share of the total population.

Elderly Growth in California

The growth of the elderly population is assured in California, just as it is in the rest of the United States, barring some unforeseen catastrophe. The only variables affecting that growth are increase in longevity and the in-migration of elderly from other states and areas. In 1985 there were 2.9 million people aged 65 or older in California. Let us see how their numbers will grow under different assumptions.

Baseline Longevity

Five-year longevity increase. A five-year increase in longevity by the year 2030 is our baseline assumption. On this assumption, the elderly would number 9.3 million by the year 2030, an absolute increase of 6.4 million over the 1985 figure. If we use our baseline assumptions about the rest of the population, the elderly would constitute 22.3 percent of the state's population.

Other Assumptions

No longevity increase. It is highly unlikely that there will be no further increases in longevity, but for an absolute floor figure, let us assume that is the case. The numbers of elderly would then increase to 8.0 million by the year 2030, an absolute increase of 5.1 million over the 1985 figure. This would put their share at 20.0 percent. Although this projection is unrealistically low, we can assume that, under normal circumstances, there will be a minimum of 8.0 million Californians age 65 or over in 2030.

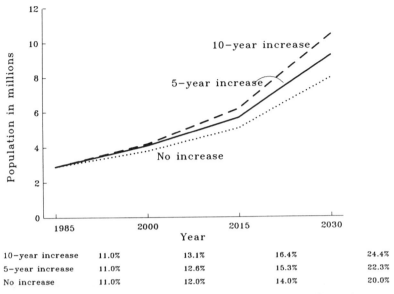

Fig. 3.11. Elderly population, California, 1985–2030, on different longevity assumptions

Ten-year longevity increase. Given the increasing emphasis on more healthful lifestyles and on geriatric research aimed at increasing life expectancy, it is not impossible that longevity could increase as much as 10 years by 2030. In that case, the elderly Californians swell to 10.5 million, representing 24.4 percent of the population. Every fourth person would be age 65 or over.

In-migration of the elderly. We have not attempted to show any effects of age-stratified in-migration. For some years now, Florida and more recently Arizona have seen a marked in-migration of elderly retirees, fleeing the snow belt to live out their remaining years in the relative warmth of the sun belt. We do not make any attempt to see how this type of elderly migration would affect the overall growth of elderly. But obviously any increase of elderly in-migrants to this state from other areas (most likely the Northeast) would cause the number of elderly to grow at an even more rapid rate.

Figure 3.11 shows the projected growth of the state's elderly population over the 1985–2030 period under different longevity assumptions.

Floor and Ceiling Considerations

In the discussion above, we have briefly presented various combinations of assumptions about fertility, migration, and mortality and their effects on the growth of the Latino and elderly populations. Some combinations, while perhaps within the realm of possibility, are not very likely for a number of reasons, which we offer here.

In our judgment the no-immigration scenario is a near impossibility. Immigration from Latin America is, to a large extent, fueled by economic differentials. Absent some radical narrowing of comparative standards of living between the United States and Latin America, immigration is certain to continue.

Likewise, we do not think there is a strong likelihood of a rapid fertility decline. Although fertility is dropping among U.S.-born Latinas, the constant addition of foreign-born newcomers of higher fertility will keep the rate up. Granted, fertility is dropping in Mexico, but the most optimistic official goal is to lower the rate to 2.1 by 2000, and that goal is conceded to be out of reach (Mexico, Consejo Nacional de Poblacion 1978). We think that the slow decline to 1.8 children per female of childbearing age by 2030 is far more likely than the rapid decline to 1.3 in 15 years.

As indicated earlier, it is nearly impossible that life expectancy will not continue to lengthen. A five-year increase by the year 2030 is reasonable; a ten-year increase is quite possible.

We see a distinct possibility of a surge in immigration, generated at some date in the mid-range future (before 2030) because of instability in Mexico. The actual magnitude is completely unforeseeable. We offer our figures only as a means of seeing the effect of a large immigration spike.

There is also a distinct possibility of increased immigration from Central America, where the destabilization induced by U.S. foreign policy has already produced a noticeable but uncounted increase in the number of immigrants. A major conflagration in the area could quickly increase the immigration figure even if Mexico were to remain stable.

While the future is impossible to predict, one can choose among alternative scenarios. In our judgment the combinations of fertility, migration, and mortality that are most likely to occur are those that will yield increased growth in both the Latino and elderly populations, thereby accentuating the age-ethnic stratification.

Other Facets of California's Population Growth

Growth in Mexico

Because immigration from Mexico is so important for the future population of California, we need to look at the demographic trends in that country. Until relatively recently Mexico had a low rate of population growth. In 1910 the population was only 15.2 million and was growing by only 1.1 percent a year. During the years 1910–20, a period of tremendous upheaval, Mexico had a growth rate of −1.5 percent. As recently as 1930 the growth rate was still only 1.1 percent (Mexico, Consejo Nacional de Poblacion 1978).

With the beginning of industrialization in 1930, however, the country's death rate fell and its growth rate climbed. By 1950 the population had almost doubled, to 27.4 million, and by 1980 it climbed to 69.4 million (see Fig. 3.12). Although the growth rate has now slowed somewhat, it is still high. Projections of Mexico's population in the year 2000, as shown in Figure 3.12, range from a high of 109.2 million to a low of 99.6 million (Mexico, Consejo Nacional de Poblacion 1982).

Growth Among Other Minorities

The two largest ethnic groups in California are, and will continue to be, the Anglos and the Latinos. However, both the Asians and the Blacks will increase their shares by 2030. In 1985 some 7.0 percent of Californians were of Asian origin. This is a population in which fertility is low, but immigration, both documented and undocumented, high. Historically, the state's Asian popula-

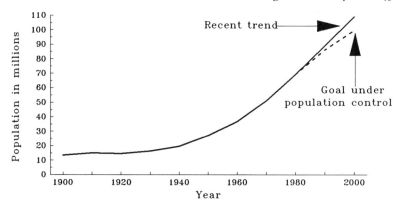

Fig. 3.12. Actual and projected population of Mexico, 1900–2000.
Sources: *1900–1970*, Secretaria de Programacion y Presupuesto, *Agenda Estadistica, 1982* (Mexico, D.F., 1983), pp. 66–67; *1980–2000*, Consejo Nacional de Poblacion, *Estimaciones y Proyecciones de Poblacion, 1950–2000* (Mexico, D.F., 1982), pp. 43, 57.

tion has been primarily of Chinese, Japanese, and Filipino ancestry. There was a substantial surge from 1978 to 1982, a period in which approximately 473,000 Southeast Asians immigrated to the United States (Gwertzman 1985). Many, if not most, of these immigrants eventually settled in California. Fertility is high in this group, but will no doubt decline. Although Southeast Asian immigration dropped off sharply after 1982, there is always the possibility of another surge at some future date. The expiration of the Hong Kong lease in the 1990's, for example, could lead to inflow from that area for a while. By our baseline model, Asians will constitute 12.5 percent of the state's population by 2030.

The Blacks' share of the state's population in 1985 was 7.8 percent. This population, as shown earlier in Figure 2.6, has low, below-replacement fertility (1.7), stereotypes to the contrary. Black foreign immigration is insignificant, and in-migration from other states, relatively high during the Second World War and the postwar years, has slowed. In our baseline projections, the Black population continues a slow, constant growth, increasing its total share to 8.8 percent.

Dependency Ratios

To discuss the potential problems of age-ethnic stratification, we shall use the concept of the *dependency ratio* (the ratio of children and seniors to the working-age population). This ratio, representing as it does an income transfer between generations, is something that policymakers must begin considering now. Decisions made today will determine whether the younger, heavily Latino population will have the economic capacity and political will to voluntarily transfer large portions of its income to a largely Anglo senior population. In this chapter we offer a framework for conceptualizing the links between generations and ethnic groups that will serve as a general organizing device for the remainder of this book.

For policy purposes, in speaking of the dependency ratio the very young (here ages 0–15) and the old (65 and over) are considered to be economically inactive and therefore dependent in some fashion on the productivity of the working-age population, ages 16–64. The dependency ratio, the total of the young and the old divided by the total working age, will be expressed in terms of the number of dependents per 1,000 working-age people. (Though strictly speaking this group simply embraces all people ages 16 to 64, for convenience, in the following pages, we shall call them "workers.")

In 1985 California's dependency ratio was 499 : 1,000; and the bulk of the dependents were children (335 vs. 164 elderly; see Fig. 3.13); otherwise stated, for every dependent aged person, there were two workers. But we find some very important differences by ethnicity within this ratio. For one thing, the Anglo population had a much higher incidence of elderly dependents than Latinos did, and a correspondingly lower incidence of children. And for another, where the Anglos' dependency ratio was slightly lower than the state ratio, the Latinos' was substantially higher. For every 1,000 Anglo workers, there were 477 Anglo dependents, and almost half of them were elderly. Latino workers were supporting 592 Latino dependents, and almost all of these were children; only 63 in 592 were elderly (see Fig. 3.14).

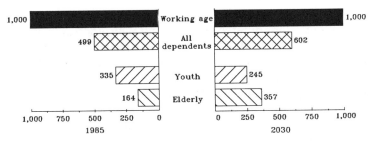

Fig. 3.13. Number of dependents per 1,000 working-age adults, California, 1985 and 2030, baseline assumptions

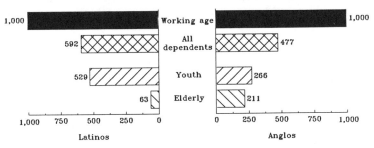

Fig. 3.14. Number of dependents per 1,000 working-age Latinos and Anglos, California, 1985

Baseline Dependency Ratios

Given the baseline assumptions, some very dramatic changes will take place in the dependent population by the year 2030. Because of the aging of the Baby Boomers, California's dependency ratio will climb to 602, an increase of nearly 21 percent over the 1985 figure (499 : 1,000). Moreover, it will be weighted very heavily toward the elderly. As Figure 3.13 shows, by then there will be 357 elderly and only 245 children per 1,000 workers, or 59.3 percent elderly dependents and 40.7 percent children. Under our baseline assumptions, the elderly dependents will begin to outnumber children around the year 2015 and will continue to outnumber them after that.

Figure 3.15 illustrates that in terms of ethnicity, there will again be some important differences. To begin with, the Anglo population's dependency ratio, which was lower than the overall ratio in 1985, will now be much higher, climbing to 699 : 1,000. And the ratio will be overwhelmingly weighted toward the elderly: only 186 of the 699 dependents will be children. Observe that, with 513 Anglo elderly per 1,000 Anglo workers, the ratio for the elderly alone will be higher than the state's *overall* dependency ratio in 1985. As for the Latinos, their ratio of dependents would actually drop to 506 : 1,000, a significant decline from the 1985 figure and well below the state's overall ratio in 2030. However, despite a substantial shift toward the elderly, that group would still be outnumbered by children (293 to 213).

Floor and Ceiling Dependency Ratios

Let us now see how different growth scenarios might change the baseline dependency ratios for 2030. In the case of a sudden cessation of Latino and all other foreign immigration after 1985, the overall dependency ratio would climb from 602 : 1,000 to 671 : 1,000. Younger immigrants would no longer enter the state, and society as a whole would become older. Thus 441 of these dependents would be elderly and only 230 children. In short, each worker would have to bear nearly half the cost of supporting an elderly person.

Such a scenario, as we have said, is beyond the realm of possibility. But the converse, as we have also said, is all too likely. Under our immigration-influx scenario, the dependency ratio for the year 2030 would fall slightly from the baseline figure, dipping to 578 : 1,000. These 578 would include somewhat fewer elderly than in the baseline case (327, down from 357) and slightly more children (251, up from 245). Both projections are illustrated in Figure 3.16.

Since a sudden immigration surge of this magnitude is a possibility, it is worth pausing a moment to consider the dependency situation in Mexico. At the moment the dependency ratio there is exceedingly high—much higher than California's. Figure 3.17 shows the ratios for both in 1985. As we see, for every 1,000 Mexi-

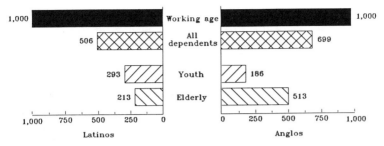

Fig. 3.15. Number of dependents per 1,000 working-age Latinos and Anglos, California, 2030

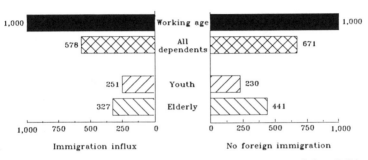

Fig. 3.16. Number of dependents per 1,000 working-age adults, California 2030, on different immigration assumptions

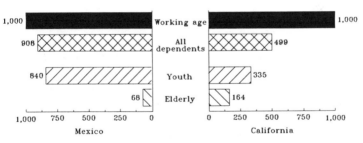

Fig. 3.17. Number of dependents per 1,000 working-age adults, Mexico and California, 1985. Source: *Mexico*, same as Fig. 3.1.

can workers, there are 908 dependents. But the more important figure, in the present context, is the proportion of children—840. Mexico is a youthful society, and historically, Mexican immigration has influenced the California ratio by weighting it toward younger dependents and away from the elderly. From this perspective, then, not only would the growth of the U.S. Latino population be beneficial; a stream of young immigrants from Mexico (and other parts of Latin America) would help to mitigate the effect of the aging of the Baby Boom generation. Besides being physically impossible, closing the border to these immigrants would, from the dependency-ratio standpoint, be extremely shortsighted.

The Intergenerational Compact

Masked in the dependency ratios is an intergenerational compact that has provided much social cohesion in the United States in the past. This compact (Keyfitz 1983) is an implicit consensus that the working-age population should provide for the young and the elderly. As the demographic changes leading to age-ethnic stratification strain society's capacity to fulfill the intergenerational compact, this consensus may dissolve. At best, new policies and programs will have to be developed if the future working-age generations are to meet this intergenerational obligation.

The Generational Claim

In order for the intergenerational compact to be fulfilled, the dependent generations must have a strong enough claim on workers that they are willing to part with a portion of what they produce. In earlier times the claim of one generation on another was private, direct, and very personal. The traditional extended family (children, parents, and grandparents living under one roof or in one small geographic area) embodied these claims; the children had the generational claim of parental love and affection, the grandparents the claim of respect, honor, and duty, if not filial affection. This was of course the ideal, and when people failed to assume their responsibilities, religious and charitable organizations attempted to fill the gap.

The claim of one generation on another is important. A break in the compact between adults and their children could mean, quite literally, the death of a society. If the claims of young children were to be ignored and their needs unattended, none would survive, and any such society would soon die out by a simple failure to replace itself. A break in the intergenerational compact between workers and their elders would be less obviously damaging to a society, but a refusal to honor the claims of the elderly would certainly cause many of their children to question their allegiance to such a society as they grew older.

Society's Carrying Capacity

If the intergenerational compact is to be honored, a society must possess two qualities. First, its workers must be economically productive enough to meet the needs of the older and younger generations. Second, those workers must have the desire to forgo part of what they produce to meet the needs of a society's dependents. Thus, both productive capacity and political will are essential to the success of the intergenerational compact.

A society's carrying capacity at any given moment is the result of earlier decisions made by prior generations. Those decisions turn above all on the degree of investment in the society's resources, both human and physical. Of the two, the human resources, represented by the younger generation, are the more important, for the ability of individuals to work together, to organize themselves effectively, and to carry out the complex technical jobs of modern economies is the prime asset of a modern society (Keyfitz 1983). Still, for those individuals to work most effectively, investments must be made in physical resources—transportation, communications, power, water, sewage, and the like are critical to efficient productivity. Any generation that ignored either set of investments would seriously impair the productive capacity of the next generation and would place in jeopardy the society's capacity to fulfill the intergenerational compact. But a generation that saw to it that its children were well educated and prepared, and that gave them a well-functioning physical structure not only would ensure the younger generation's economic carrying capacity, but would also have a very strong intergenerational claim on it (Keyfitz 1983).

Current Trends

A society seeking to ensure its future carrying capacity must focus policy attention on the human and physical resource needs of the younger generation. Programs for the elderly are hardly an investment in future productivity, but only a repayment for past participation. Yet if we look at the trajectories of current social policy, it appears that society has decided to invest in the elderly and to defer investment in the young. On a per-capita basis, governmental expenditure on the elderly increased significantly between 1973 and 1983, continuing a trend that has been evident since 1960 (Preston 1984; Petersen 1982a,b). Meanwhile, programs that benefit the younger generations, particularly children, have suffered significant per-capita drops.

This discrepancy between the benefits received by the elderly and the young may be best appreciated by considering the results of the principal public programs that serve the two groups—education and health care. Nationally, education expenditures have yielded a negative outcome; that is, for whatever level of expenditure, the young are less well educated now than they were 20 years ago. The rate of high school graduation has dropped noticeably, from 76.3 percent in 1965 to 73.6 percent in 1980 (Preston 1984: 45). Scores on the Scholastic Aptitude Test dropped by nearly 90 points between 1963 and 1980. For Latinos, as we will see in a later chapter, the educational outcomes were even worse. California has seen a drop in interest in education and has fallen near the bottom of the country in per-capita expenditures. The elderly, on the other hand, seem to be in better and better health each year. Nationally, longevity has increased steadily (Rice & Feldman 1982; Preston 1984: 46) and considerable research, social as well as medical, is given to the study of their problems.

What this means is that the education and social service needs of the young are increasingly being left to the decaying nuclear family to provide, while the expensive needs of the elderly are increasingly assumed by the public. The fate of the elderly rests not in the hands of their own children, but in public policy. In a sense the elderly are insulated from the vagaries of their children's economic position by social policy. The young, particularly in the areas of education and health care, on the other hand, appear to have less and less call on public monies, and may turn only to their biological parents for support (Preston 1984: 49).

For the purposes of this book, we have not focused on the mechanics of the intergenerational compact: the support needs of the elderly are taken as an aggregate need that must be met by the younger generation of society. Currently, much of this need is met by federal programs (Anderson & Hager 1981; Anderson et al. 1983). However, these programs may be easily made a state responsibility, and perhaps just as easily a county responsibility. No matter which level of jurisdiction—federal, state, county— passes the buck, it will stop with the younger generation. And when the buck stops, the burden will be quite heavy.

This national intergenerational picture can only become exacerbated when applied to the age-ethnic stratified society of California. The needs of Latino children may easily be pushed aside by the needs of the publicly supported Anglo elderly. The Latino working-age person indeed will have difficult decisions to make. Those decisions will be heavily colored by the treatment he or she has received at the hands of society in the next years. It is to this subject that we now turn.

The Interethnic Compact

Discussion of the intergenerational compact in California must take into account the impending age-ethnic stratification. As we have seen in Figure 3.13, under the baseline assumptions the state's dependency ratio is projected to grow from 499 : 1,000 in 1985 to 602 : 1,000 in 2030, by which time the greater share of dependents will be elderly people, not children. By then the dependent generations will be composed of very different ethnic groups: the children will be nearly half Latino (and about two-thirds minority), while a majority of the elderly will be Anglo (see Fig. 3.7). The Latinos and Anglos will be nearly equally represented in a working-age population that will be 60 percent minority.

In these circumstances, two questions pose themselves. What claim will the great numbers of Anglo elderly have on the Latino and minority workers? And, How will the intergenerational compact between the working-age and the elderly generations be fulfilled when they are of a very different ethnic composition?

Recall the two qualities we discussed as requisite to the fulfilling of the intergenerational compact: the *will* to fulfill it and the *resources*, primarily human resources, to fulfill it. Whether the Latino and minority workers of 2030 are willing and able to transfer large portions of their income to support the population of Anglo elderly depends on the intergenerational and interethnic decisions now being made at the lower end of the age spectrum. Let us turn the question around. It is a mirror image of the others: Is the largely Anglo, working-age Baby Boom generation of 1985 willing to dedicate a sufficient portion of its economic pie to an investment in the Latino and minority youth of today?

What we are proposing is that thought and discussion about the *intergenerational compact* must be accompanied by thought and discussion about a new concept: the *interethnic compact*. Society as a whole must commit itself to ensuring the full participation of all ethnic groups at every occupational and social level. Less-than-complete participation should be seen not just as a problem to be confronted by one group, but as society's problem.

There are structural reasons why Latinos and other minorities are not participating fully today. If this situation is to be remedied, the education and health of Latino and minority children must be seen as society's responsibility, and the full productivity and representation of Latinos and minorities at every occupational level must be the goal of all.

All this implies a massive change in attitudes as well as policies. Not only has there never been an interethnic compact in California; historically, there has often been something approaching ethnic war. From the anti-Mexican Foreign Miners' Tax of 1850, through the Chinese exclusion acts of the late nineteenth century, the Mexican deportations of the 1930's, and the Japanese internments of the 1940's, to the current complaints about "illegal" immigrants and bilingual education, the state's Anglo population has rarely shown itself to be much concerned about establishing a positive relationship with the various ethnic groups in its midst. But with the emergence of an age-ethnic stratified population, the intergenerational compact will quickly take on the flavor of an implicit interethnic compact. The political implications of this transformation are serious indeed, for a failure to seal that compact will impair the future of the intergenerational compact.

Given California's wealth and the state's tremendous economic growth in the mid- to late 1980's, the question of whether today's workers have the wherewithal to invest in the younger generation scarcely needs to be asked. Proportionately, the economic burden of youth has diminished substantially from the levels during the 1950's and 1970's. The question that *does* need to be asked is that of will. When faced with a choice between pursuing an affluent "Yuppie" lifestyle that consumes many resources and deferring part of that gratification to invest in a young generation that is very different ethnically, how will the Baby Boomers respond?

One can imagine a scenario in which the Baby Boom generation chooses to use the fruits of its economic success to indulge itself, so that little would remain to invest in the human and physical resources of following generations. In such a case, the elderly Baby Boomers would have little claim on those who follow them. One can, however, just as easily imagine a scenario in which the current working-age generation does invest in the Latino and minority younger generations now, thereby enabling them to fulfill the intergenerational compact as they mature and enter the labor force.

There are many impediments to a decision to invest in the youth of today, not least the majority Anglos' perception of the young minorities among them as different, bothersome, and unapproachable. Because of this perception, the easiest policy route would be to continue on as we are, ignoring the needs of these young people and investing most of our available resources in such areas as geriatric research. But it is also a dangerous route. Do we really want to prolong life at the risk of a break in the intergenerational compact?

An interethnic compact, though difficult to develop, is not an impossibility. It will require a change in people's perceptions (and misconceptions); it will require the working-out and adoption of a long-range generational policy that can transcend the short-range political interest of elected officials; and it will require the involvement of the private sector.

Chapter Four

Employment and Income

From the demographic trends, it is clear enough that, whatever policy is devised, the workers of the early twenty-first century will be called on to assume a substantially larger support burden. Over the period 2015 to 2030 California's working-age population will increase by only 590,000 (or 2.2%) as the elderly's numbers swell by 3.6 million (or 63%). One has to worry more than a little about the work force's capacity to generate sufficient income to shoulder that burden.

The basic requirement of an income-transfer mechanism is that there be sufficient income to transfer. In addition, non-cash support programs require a funding base. In this chapter we consider the employment and income status of Latinos vis-à-vis the rest of the population. With a quick glance at potential future unearned income needs, we shall be in a position to identify some major policy areas that will require attention in the immediate future.

The Income Gap

In 1980 Latino income in California was about two-thirds Anglo income. The average income for a Latino family was $18,670, compared with an Anglo value of $26,720. Asian income, at $24,400, was nearly as high as the Anglos', but Black family income, at $18,220, was even lower than the Latinos (see Fig. 4.1).

For California we estimate that of the $321 billion total income in 1985, Latinos, 21 percent of the population, generated $40 billion, or 12 percent of the total; that Anglos, 64 percent of the population, generated $244 billion, or 76 percent; and that Asians

TABLE 4.1

Income by Ethnicity and Sex as a Percent of Anglo Male Income, California,
1950–1980

Category	1950	1960	1970	1980
Anglo female	47.9%	46.1%	45.4%	47.9%
Black male	68.2	62.2	63.1	67.0
Black female	37.5	31.9	38.6	47.6
Asian male	61.3	71.0	77.6	76.5
Asian female	45.8	35.8	42.1	45.9
Latino male	69.5	69.9	68.8	62.1
Latino female	37.4	34.1	32.9	34.7

SOURCE: California Employment Development Department, *Socio-Economic Trends in California, 1940–1980* (Sacramento, 1986), p. 57.

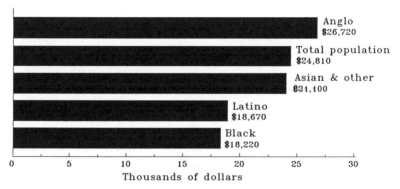

Fig. 4.1. Average family income by ethnicity, California, 1979. Source: California Employment Development Department, *Socio-Economic Trends in California, 1940–1980* (Sacramento, 1986), p. 59.

and Blacks, 15 percent of the population, accounted for $37 billion, or 12 percent.

This income differential is not a recent phenomenon. Data from the 1950, 1960, 1970, and 1980 censuses show a persistent and, indeed, widening gap between Anglo and Latino incomes. Taking Anglo male income in any year as equal to 100 percent, we find that Latino male income actually fell by over 7 percentage points in that period (see Table 4.1). The income of Latino females also dropped, though less sharply, as did Anglo female income. Black male and Asian female income dipped and rose, so that in 1980 both groups were earning approximately the same amount relative to Anglo male income as in 1950. The only groups whose incomes improved relative to the Anglo males were Black females and Asian males. By and large the period 1950–80 was one of tremendous economic growth, but clearly all groups did not benefit equally from that growth.

Income may be generated from various sources. We have defined *earned income* as the money gained from current employment. *Unearned income* is cash income from income-transfer mechanisms such as Social Security, welfare payments, and unemployment benefits. *IDR* income is the money from interest, dividends, and rentals, and is primarily the result of earlier investment efforts.

In Figure 4.2 we see that in 1985 the sources of Latino income were markedly different from the sources of Anglo income. In both cases the majority of income was earned: 87 percent for Latinos and 76 percent for Anglos. A slightly smaller portion of the Latinos' income was unearned but the difference is minor. The major difference was in the income from interest, dividends, and rentals, which accounted for only 2.5 percent of Latino income against fully 11.4 percent for the Anglos.

The structural differences between Latino and Anglo economic participation are here strikingly revealed, for though both Latinos and Anglos earn most of their income and draw roughly the same amount from unearned sources, Anglo IDR income is about 4.5 times more likely than Latino IDR income. In essence, Latinos are not receiving investment income from the California economy; hence they must work for wages. This lack of investment indicates one area in need of policy consideration.

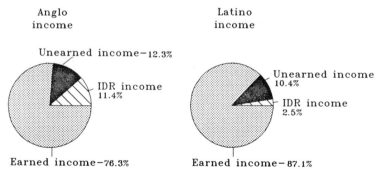

Fig. 4.2. Sources of Anglo and Latino income, California, 1985

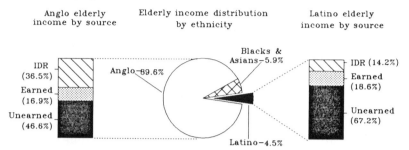

Fig. 4.3. Distribution of elderly income by ethnicity showing sources of elderly income for Anglos and Latinos, California, 1985

Even greater income differences are found among people 65 and over (see Fig. 4.3). In 1985 elderly income amounted to $41 billion. Anglos, who represented 83 percent of the group, received $36.7 billion, or about 90 percent of the total. Latinos, who were 8 percent of the elderly, received $1.8 billion, or less than 5 percent of elderly income. On a per-capita basis, Anglo elderly received $15,333 per person, Latinos less than half as much—$6,380.

A major difference, and perhaps an explanation of the disparity in total amounts, may again be found in the IDR income figures. Both Latino and Anglo elderly receive approximately the same proportion of earned income. But the Latinos received less than 15 percent of their income from interest, dividends, and rentals, compared with almost 37 percent for the Anglos. Accordingly, the Latino elderly are much more dependent on unearned income (67.2%, compared with 46.6% for the Anglos).

This difference, though troubling, does not loom large as an issue at the moment, since there are so few Latinos among the elderly. More important are two other issues: Latino participation in the labor force and the need of *all* the elderly for non-earned income as their numbers grow.

Latino Labor Force Participation

Latinos are willing to work. One measure of this is their rate of participation in the labor force, which is based on those who are either employed or seeking employment. In California Latinos have consistently been slightly more active participants than other groups (see Appendix Table A.6 for the rates for 1940–80). Fully 80.6 percent of Latino working-age males were in the labor force in 1980, compared with 76.1 percent of all males. The participation rate for Latinas was substantially the same as for all females (roughly 52 percent).

This rate of participation is the more remarkable considering that Latinos are likely to find themselves in jobs of short duration, with frequent periods of unemployment. Yet Latino workers have the shortest period of unemployment between jobs, an average of 7.4 weeks, compared with 8.6 for Anglos and 9.7 for Blacks (EDD 1981).

From the standpoint of effort, then, the Latino worker is one of the most active and assertive elements in the California labor market. Yet the willingness to work that is brought to the marketplace is generally not rewarded commensurately. The higher-skill, higher-income occupations rarely have full Latino participation. There is in fact a very obvious occupational skewing. Very few Latinos work in any of the higher-level occupations. As we see in Figure 4.4, only 3.6 percent of medical professionals in 1980 were Latinos. They accounted for just 1.8 percent of the state's physicians and only 5.6 percent of the nurses. Other professions show similar levels of underrepresentation. Of lawyers and judges, 3.6 percent were Latino; of natural scientists 4.5 percent; of engineers and architects 5.1 percent; of postsecondary teachers 5.8 percent; of executives and managers 7.0 percent; of primary and secondary school teachers 7.9 percent. And looking down the list, we find Latinos concentrated at the low end of the occupational scale, accounting for 70.7 percent of all farmworkers, 41.6 percent of assemblers and handworkers, 32.9 percent of laborers, and 28.9 percent of cleaning and building service workers.

The reasons for this degree of maldistribution can easily be traced to serious problems at the early stages of education and training. For example, take the Latinos' low representation among physicians. Though very few Latinos study and practice medicine in California, there is nothing inherent in Mexican or Latin American culture that inhibits the study of medicine. On the contrary, Mexico has more students of medicine, both absolutely and per capita, than any other major country. With a population of over

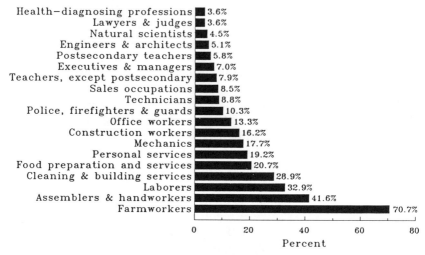

Fig. 4.4. Occupational distribution of Latinos, California, 1980. Source: U.S. Bureau of the Census, *Census of Population, 1980: Equal Employment Opportunity Special File* (Washington, D.C., 1982).

70 million in 1980, Mexico had 87,000 medical students, compared with about 40,000 in the United States, a country with three times as many people (Lopez Acuna 1982: 149). Mexico is thus training nearly seven times as many physicians per capita as the United States.

The situation is the same at the other high occupational levels. Large numbers of engineers, lawyers, teachers, and executives are trained in Mexico and Latin America, but we find few Latinos being trained for these occupations in California.

Future Labor Market Changes

Two important trends are affecting the labor force of the near future: the growth of the service and high-technology sector and the shrinking of the number of Anglos entering the work force.

California's high-technology sector is an area that may hold the key to future economic growth. Ideas, rather than tangible products, may well be the major source of future economic growth

(Kelley 1982). The educational level of the future work force is therefore of prime importance. Only a well-educated labor force can function productively and competitively in this sector (Gardner 1984; Carlson 1982).

The second trend we have already touched on: the number of Anglos entering the labor market is decreasing and will continue to do so. Some industries in California in fact are already experiencing labor shortages of one sort or another (Kaufman 1982). Without high Latino fertility and immigration, there could be serious shortages in a matter of decades. Some observers have proposed that drastic measures will be needed, speculating even that foreigners might have to be hired as military personnel (Butz et al. 1982).

These trends will combine with others we have examined to work important changes in the labor force of the future. Our projections on the direction of change in the state's future labor force and income-generating ability are based on the following sets of assumptions.

1. Overall population change as in the baseline population model: a five-year increase in longevity; a slow decline in Latino fertility; and an annual in-migration of 250,000 people, of which 100,000 will be Latino.

2. Increasing participation by all females. This affects Latinos more than any other group, for Latinas currently participate at slightly lower levels than any minority female group. Female participation has been increasing since 1940, and in our basic labor-force participation model, we assume that trend will continue until, by 2030, approximately 30 percent more of the female population will be participating than in 1985.

3. Declining labor-force participation by seniors at age 65. The values for these assumptions are given in Table 4.2.

4. Real (non-inflationary) per-worker income growth of 1 percent per year. This growth rate is above that experienced during the 1960's and 1970's.

Our projections indicate that the labor force will change in important ways. By 2030 the overall labor force will be 42 percent larger than in 1985, growing to 19.8 million. However, as Figure 4.5 shows, almost all this growth occurs before 2015. In the subse-

TABLE 4.2
Elderly Labor-Force Participation, California, 1940–1980
(Percent of all elderly)

Elderly	1940	1950	1960	1970	1980
Employed	19.2%	17.7%	16.6%	14.0%	11.9%
Unemployed	1.6	1.4	1.4	0.9	0.8
Labor-force					
participation	20.8	19.1	18.0	14.9	12.7

SOURCE: Same as Table 4.1, p. 33.

quent years the labor force adds only 300,000 workers, a total increase (amounting to less than 2 percent over the entire period of 15 years) that is substantially less than the *annual* growth of the labor force during the years 1980–85.

This sharply reduced rate of growth is a result of the shrinking Anglo labor pool. Looking at Figure 4.5, we see that the number of Anglo workers grows slowly, from 9.4 million in 1985 to 10.0 million in 2000, and that from this peak their numbers begin to decline, until by 2030 there are fewer Anglo workers than there were in 1980 (8.4 million). What keeps the labor force growing, then, is the Latino labor pool, which keeps on expanding over the entire period, to number 7.2 million workers by 2030. In percentage terms, Latinos increase their share of the labor force from 18.8 percent to 34.9 percent between 1985 and 2030, while the Anglo share falls from 66.9 percent to 44.6 percent. Clearly, the Latino workers will play an increasingly important role in the state's economy.

Elderly Income Needs

As we saw in Chapters 2 and 3, according to our baseline population model, the number of people aged 65 and over will more than triple between 1985 and 2030, from 2.9 million to 9.3 million. We have spoken generally of dependency ratios and income transfer. It is now time to look more closely at what the support of these people implies for the working population. We shall speak in terms of the aggregate need of the elderly in the state, without reference to any particular level of government or private activity.

And we shall confine our discussion to cash benefits. Non-cash benefits, primarily services provided, such as medical services (financed currently under Medicare), housing, social support, and attendant care, are simply not included. How does an analyst measure the relative cost of an older person spending a pleasant afternoon in the comfort and safety of a senior center? Thus, the most that can be said is that with a tripling of the elderly, the cost of these services will assuredly be heavy—as a rule of thumb, in fact, the essential non-cash benefits alone (primarily health-care services) may be as large a cost burden as the cash benefits—and must be somehow paid for by the working-age population.

The cash benefits are easier to identify. These may be traced as part of the overall cash income of the elderly. On the basis of current income data, we can therefore project what the future cash-benefit support burden might be. We begin by looking at unearned income. Our projections have assumed a real per-capita income growth rate of 1 percent per annum. This assumption suggests the elderly's income "needs" include increases in their standard of living comparable to worker productivity increases.

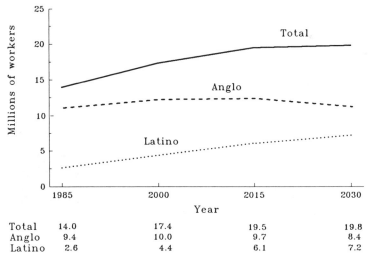

	1985	2000	2015	2030
Total	14.0	17.4	19.5	19.8
Anglo	9.4	10.0	9.7	8.4
Latino	2.6	4.4	6.1	7.2

Fig. 4.5. Size of total, Anglo, and Latino labor forces, California, 1985–2030

Whether the elderly income "needs" can be realized is a central issue—it is the economic aspect of the burden of support.

In 1985 the elderly in California received $20 billion of the state's unearned income. Assuming a 1985 level of benefits and a sharply declining labor-force participation after age 65 (i.e., retirement), the demand for unearned income will grow gradually through 2010, at which point it will more than double, to $43 billion. But as the Baby Boomers begin to turn 65, the demand for unearned income will increase sharply, reaching $106 billion by 2030—a five-fold increase over the 1985 figure (see Fig. 4.6). When broken down by ethnicity, the Anglo elderly (58.5% of the total elderly in 2030) will receive 63.8 percent of the unearned income; the Latino elderly, though 22.5 percent of the total, will receive only 19.6 percent. In short, under our model the majority of the elderly in 2030 will be Anglos, and they will receive nearly two-thirds of the unearned income required by this group.

In 1985 the elderly received very little of their income from earnings: barely $7.1 billion (17.3%). Assuming no major changes in this trend, earned income will almost double, to $13.8 billion by 2030, when it will have dropped to 7.9 percent of all elderly income.

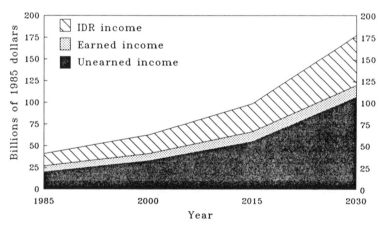

Fig. 4.6. Sources of elderly income, California, 1985–2030

But the elderly's demand for IDR income will grow much more substantially. Income from previous investment will quadruple, climbing from $14.0 billion in 1985 to $57.1 billion by 2030 (see Tables A.14 and A.15). These projections also include a 1 percent per annum increase per capita—once again assuming a standard-of-living increase for the elderly commensurate with the increase in worker productivity. As we have seen, the Anglo elderly will receive the vast share of this type of income, 85.9 percent.

To pull these figures together, we project that the elderly will require $175 billion by the year 2030, or to put it another way, a 428 percent growth of income. Of this total, Anglos will receive 72 percent, Latinos 16 percent, and other minorities 12 percent. Above all, the need for elderly unearned income would increase—by 532 percent, according to our projections. Under these conditions the Anglo majority will receive a disproportionate share of this income and a greatly disproportionate share of IDR income.

The massive amounts of disinvestment required for the elderly during the 2010-to-2030 period as they liquidate their earlier private-sector investments will have significant effects on securities markets and corporate profitability. That the IDR income needs of the elderly will be realizable is unlikely. A dramatic decline in securities market prices because of such enormous disinvestment during this period is probable.

Income-Generating Potential of the Future Labor Force

We have examined what the labor force of 2030 is likely to look like and what the cost of supporting the elderly promises to be. The question now is: Will that labor force be capable of bearing that cost?

We have added to the basic labor-force model two additional assumptions to give an income projection. These are, first, that current income differentials will continue, and second, that the real productivity of all workers will grow at a projected rate of 1 percent per year per worker. Under these assumptions, let us look at the shifting income picture as the number of elderly triples and the Latino population grows by two and one-half times.

To begin with, the state's total income, preserving 1985 differentials in income by population group, rises from $320 billion in 1985 to $804 billion by 2030. Whereas the labor force increases by 42 percent, total income increases by 251 percent. Much of this increase, however, is due to our factoring in an overall income growth (in 1985 dollars) of 1 percent a year. A more discriminating indicator is the amount of earned income generated. This figure rises from $251.1 billion to $536.9 billion by 2030, an increase of 214 percent.

Such an increase, it is clear, is not commensurate with the predicted 532 percent increase in demand for elderly unearned income. This is the area of greatest concern, for such a demand may well place strains on the society's income-redistributing capacity.

The ratio of total earned income to unearned elderly income tells the story: in 1985 that ratio was $12.57 to $1.00 (hereafter stated as a pure ratio, i.e. 12.57 : 1). By 2030 it will drop to 5.06 : 1.

Our income projections are only a preliminary toe-in-the-water estimate. To develop any sense at all of what might happen, we have adopted a stance of *ceteris paribus* on the macro scale. That is, for this run of projections, we have had to assume there will be no major shift in economic activity and no new developments that will either reduce the number of jobs or dramatically increase productivity. We have assumed there will be no major negative changes in the role of the California economy relative to the rest of the U.S. economy and the economies of the Pacific Rim. We have assumed no major depression or periods of runaway inflation. In short, these income projections are done within the context of a relatively stable, modestly growing economy. Reality, of course, tends to be nonlinear and nonstable. Since our focus is on the population changes occurring within the state and their implications for social policy today, we feel that our ends will be best served by projecting today's labor-force participation and productivity trends into the future. Alternative assumptions are made in different scenarios, which serve to sensitize us to areas that need attention.

Alternative Scenarios

As with demographic trends, our projections of employment and income are based on assumptions that may or may not prove valid. We have carried forward the analysis using different assumptions to help gain an understanding of the importance of various assumptions and at the same time point to areas where public policy might profitably evolve.

Immigration Influx

Under the immigration-influx scenario discussed in Chapter 2, we assume a sudden injection over 10 years of five million immigrants from Mexico and other parts of Latin America, followed by a return to an annual Latino immigration of 100,000. Let us explore the effects of this not-unlikely possibility on labor-force size and income.

Assuming such an immigration influx, the overall size of the labor force would be 23.5 million in 2030, an increase of 3.7 million workers over the baseline figure (see Fig. 4.7). This larger labor force would be 46.4 percent Latino, 35.7 percent Anglo, and 17.8 percent other minorities.

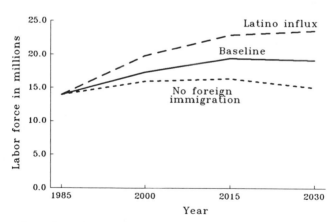

Fig. 4.7. Size of total labor force, California, 1985–2030, on different immigration assumptions

This expanded labor force would generate a total income of $912.8 billion, a jump of $108.8 billion above the baseline figure (see Table A.18).

We may now see some additional areas for policy attention. Although the labor force increases 18.7 percent under this immigration-influx assumption, total income rises only 13.5 percent. Three factors are at work here: age, ethnicity, and nativity. The immigrant-influx population is younger, Latino, and foreign-born—each factor causing income to be below average. So though total income is higher than in the baseline projection, it does not grow in direct proportion to the growth of the labor force. The pie is larger, but there will be more people sharing it. Latinos, 46.4 percent of the labor force and 45.4 percent of the population, will receive only 35.0 percent of the total income.

Adding more Latinos to the labor force would have the effect of increasing total *earned income* by a significant amount. It would rise to $620 billion, a gain of $83.6 billion, or 16.9 percent over the baseline figure.

Because of the youth of the populations of Mexico and other Latin American countries and of the Latino population in this country, a large influx of Latinos in 1990–99 does not increase the projected number of elderly in 2030 appreciably. They would grow only from 9.3 million in the baseline model to 10.2 million, a 9 percent change. This would have the effect of increasing the demand for elderly unearned income somewhat, from the $106.2 billion in the baseline model to $115.4 billion. But this increase would be more than offset by the gains in total income. The ratio of earned income to elderly unearned income would be 5.38 : 1, a slightly more favorable ratio than the 5.06 : 1 posited in the baseline model.

What are the implications of such a sudden, brief increase in immigration from Mexico or Central America? Because of the regressive structure of Social Security taxes, the major beneficiaries might well be the elderly: the addition of Latinos to the labor force would create additional earned income to offset more of the elderly's unearned income needs. An immigration influx, assuming current income differentials, would generate an additional $50.9 billion of earned income. The ability of society to transfer the income to the elderly would thus be enhanced by increased Latino participation in the labor force. A hardship would fall on the Latino population, however, for their per-capita earnings actually shrink.

No Immigration

As we have said, we think the assumption of no foreign immigration an implausible one. Nonetheless, the importance of immigration to the future of California may be more fully appreciated by seeing what effects such a cutoff would have on the state's labor force and income.

Under this assumption the overall labor force grows very slowly, eventually reaching 15 million by 2030, a gain of only 7.0 percent (1.0 million workers) in the 45-year period (see Table A.19). A majority of the workers would be Anglo (55.8%), but the Latinos' share would have increased considerably, rising from 18.6 percent in 1985 to 26.8 percent in 2030. Shutting off foreign immigration, in sum, would cut the labor force by a quarter from what it would be under the immigration assumed in our baseline model (see Fig. 4.7).

The resulting smaller population would generate only $673.9 billion of total income, about $130.1 billion less than in our baseline model. A problem will be seen immediately in the matter of earned income, which rises to only $430.5 billion in 2030 with the smaller labor force. This is $106.4 billion below the amount in our baseline model.

The labor force would be supporting about 7.0 percent fewer elderly people than under the baseline assumptions, so the need for unearned income would drop slightly, to $99.9 billion, a fall of about 5.9 percent. But because of the proportionately larger numbers of elderly, the labor force would be harder pressed to meet that need. The ratio of total earned income to elderly unearned income would drop to 4.30 : 1.

This scenario has the most serious implications of all for the future. The growing population of elderly functions as a sort of drag anchor on the rest of the population. If the borders were sealed, workers would be increasingly hard put to provide support for their seniors. An increase in immigration, as under the immigration-influx assumption, would generate $238.9 billion more in total income than would a work force with no immigrants. And even the low level of immigration in our baseline model would boost the total income by $130.1 billion over the no-immigration assumption. Clearly, the overall income picture for the state is very much affected by the inclusion of Latino immigrants.

High Achievement

In Table 4.1 we illustrated the extent of the large and persistent gap between the incomes of Anglo male workers and all others. In what we call a high-achievement simulation, we investigated what would happen if income levels of Latinos, other minorities, and females were made to correspond to those of Anglo males by age group. In other words, let us suppose that by 2030 this gap has been fully closed.

In terms of total income this would have dramatic beneficial consequences, both for the state and for its individual residents. Under the assumptions of our baseline population model (of constant but low-level immigration and slowly declining fertility), total income would rise to $1.37 trillion! This amount is $570.7 billion more than the baseline figure (see Table A.17), a huge increase in the overall pie. Earned income would also increase dramatically, to $898.0 billion, $361.1 billion over the baseline model. But comparatively speaking, the unearned income needs of the elderly would rise only moderately, to $153.6 billion. This increase would be more than offset by the marked increase in total earned income.

A work force in which all minorities and women were fully productive would thus be enormously beneficial to the California economy. It is in the best interests of the state to have an expanded labor force in which all earn their full share. This represents a classic "win-win" situation, with society as a whole much better for the change.

Changing Productivity

Our baseline analysis assumed a real per-unit income growth rate of 1 percent per year. Under this assumption elderly per-capita

TABLE 4.3
Elderly Per-Capita Total Income, California, 2030, on Different Assumptions
(Income in constant 1985 dollars)

Simulation	Maximum level: proportionate real growth	Minimum level: portion of work income
Baseline	$18,854	$9,303
No foreign immigration	19,292	8,225
Latino influx	18,457	9,767
Delayed retirement	20,123	12,958
High achievement	31,699	16,069
Low fertility	18,854	8,836
High life expectancy	18,842	8,467
Low life expectancy	18,832	10,456
No productivity increase	12,048	5,945
High productivity increase	23,545	11,618
Very high productivity increase	29,372	14,494

income would grow to over $18,800 per year by 2030. To understand the importance of this assumption, we investigated the implications of no real productivity growth and a higher rate of productivity growth.

Under a condition of no real productivity growth (see Table 4.3), changes in income would derive solely from changes in the age, sex, and ethnic mix of the work force and the ways in which their respective productive capacities would affect elderly income. Should this occur, elderly income would drop to $12,048 per year in 2030, or $6,800 less than the baseline projection and $2,200 below 1985 levels. Should productivity increase 1.5 percent per year, the elderly would be better off, with a per-capita total income of $23,545. A rate of 2 percent per annum would mean $29,372 per year. Clearly, increased productivity translates into a substantially higher standard of living, when compounded over many years.

Changing Fertility and Mortality

We also investigated the effects on income of alternative trends in fertility and life expectancy. Because we assume elderly per-capita growth tracks along at the same rate as for workers, the income effects of these changes are negligible, and per-capita elderly income in 2030 remains at about $18,000, the same as for the baseline simulation (see Tables A.20–A.22 for detailed results of these simulations).

Five-Year Delay in Retirement

One frequently mentioned policy solution to the burden-of-support problem is to increase the age of retirement. We examine here the results of a simulation in which the retirement age is raised to 70. For a rough approximation of dwindling participation due to aging alone, we have assumed that the 65–69 age cohort will participate at the same rate as the 60–64 cohort (see Tables A.8 and A.16).

With a five-year deferment in retirement, total income would increase to $815.8 billion in 2030. This is $11.8 billion more than the baseline figure, an increase of slightly less than 1.5 percent. And with people remaining in the work force longer, earned income would reach $566.8 billion, $29.9 billion (or about 5.6%) over the baseline. Plainly, the goal of reducing the support burden of the elderly would be met. The amount of unearned income needed would fall to $157.1 billion, $15.6 billion (about 8.9%) less than in the baseline model. Note, however, that the historical trend shows that the labor-force participation of the elderly population is decreasing rather than increasing (see Table 4.2).

Potential Elderly Income Shortfall

Our income analysis thus far has reflected an assumption that is not likely—specifically, that the elderly cohorts are able to dramatically increase their share of what is produced with elderly real per-capita income keeping pace with worker income growth. This means a larger and larger tax burden on workers.

An alternative hypothesis is that the elderly as a group receive a constant share of the aggregate income pie. As with the previous analysis, the total pie will change depending on the size, composition, and productivity of the work force. However, a larger number of elderly persons would result in proportionally lower total per-capita income for the elderly.

The comparative effects of this second set of alternatives are shown in Table 4.3. Column 1 shows the maximum level of elderly per-capita income for each simulation based on the assumption of proportionate real growth. This is contrasted in the second column, which shows the minimum level based on a constant portion of aggregate work income. For reference, average 1985 senior per-capita income was about $14,000.

As may be seen in the table, under baseline conditions elderly per-capita income would grow by 33 percent to $18,854 by 2030; this, however, is an unrealistic maximum. Under the adverse conditions where elderly as a group receive a fixed share of total income, the figure would fall to $9,303, or two-thirds of the 1985 level—a very dramatic decline in the elderly standard of living. Furthermore, under this adverse assumption real elderly per-capita income falls from 1985 levels, for all alternatives except for the unlikely cases of either all workers achieving male Anglo productivity levels or a real-income growth rate of 2 percent per annum.

Which condition is more likely, the maximum or the minimum? Unfortunately, we may be headed for the worst-of-all-worlds for the elderly. Specifically, elderly real income may rise dramatically until 2010 or so as productivity advances outrace the growth of the elderly cohort and as the financial markets boom from retirement-directed savings. Then, between 2010 and 2030, real elderly per-capita income may plummet as the mass of Baby Boomers retire and the financial markets collapse.

Policy Areas for Consideration

Our projections indicate several areas in need of policy attention. Before we enumerate them, let us sum up the findings. To begin with, it is clear that the size of California's future labor force is very sensitive to Latino demographics. The various projections for Latino labor-force participation in 2030 range from an unlikely low of 4.0 million to a baseline figure of 7.2 million to a high of 10.9 million. The Anglo labor force is not likely to change much under any circumstances. Therefore, labor-force size depends on

Latino demographic behavior. And the support of the elderly in turn depends on the size and productivity of the labor force.

An absence of immigrant Latinos in the work force would deprive the state of much-needed income over the next 45 years. The labor force would actually shrink just at the time the Baby Boomers are joining the ranks of the elderly. A modest amount of immigration provides a somewhat better total income picture. Although as a group Latinos would receive less than their share of income by current trends, there would be more earned income to supply the unearned income needs of the elderly. And an increased flow of migration would create even greater total income, with more money to be transferred as unearned income to the elderly. If Latinos (and all other groups) were to achieve income parity with the Anglo male workers, the income growth would be still greater, with both the elderly and the Latinos receiving larger portions of a larger pie. For the state as a whole, then, the best scenario would be increased migration in conjunction with a rise in average income of females and minority males to Anglo male levels.

Turning now to our findings on the elderly's future income needs, let us assume that our baseline model provides a realistic projection. It puts the demand for elderly unearned income in 2030 at $106.2 billion. If immigration were to remain constant, but all incomes were to equal the level of Anglo males by 2030, earned income would increase by $361.1 billion over the baseline; that increase alone would obviously more than suffice to meet the unearned income needs of the elderly. Finally, with a cessation of immigration, there would be a net loss of $106.4 billion in earned income, the full amount of the elderly's income needs; obviously, the support of the elderly would be much more problematic than it would be under the baseline model.

These findings point to four policy areas that should be of concern to all.

1. Immigration. The role of immigrants, particularly from Mexico and Central America and whether documented or undocumented, in the California labor force has been a hotly discussed issue in recent years. Our study indicates that immigration is a key factor in the dilemma of supporting the elderly. Foreign im-

migration can work to offset the otherwise inevitable shrinking of the labor force after 2010.

2. Education, employment, and income. Much of California's enormous growth in employment and income in the past four decades is due to the increased educational attainment of the work force since the Second World War. But the gains have not been spread evenly: in 1980 Anglo workers had a median of 13.3 years of schooling, compared with a median of 9.2 among male Latinos, a full four years less, and only 8.9 among Latino females. The next chapter will deal with the reasons for this educational gap. Here we need merely note that the productivity of the labor force is very sensitive to education. Accordingly, from a purely economic point of view, the state should make investment in training and education the highest priority.

3. Occupational distribution. To a great extent, this educational gap is reflected in the skewed occupational distribution of Latinos, a disparity that can only hurt the state in the long run. Efforts are needed in three key areas, if this maldistribution is to be righted. The first, obviously, is education. In recent years, great strides have been made in two of the highest-level occupations, the medical and dental fields, showing that it is possible to rapidly increase Latino participation in a highly skilled area requiring much training and knowledge. But this is only a start on the problem. The second area for work is institutional discrimination. Institutional barriers, present in both the public sector and the private sector, must be removed to ensure complete Latino participation at all levels. Finally, the energy, vision, and perseverance brought to California by immigrant Latinos should be appreciated and harnessed, not frustrated and rejected. Immigrants almost by definition have a great drive to achieve. Encouraging the Latino workers, foreign-born and native-born alike, to redouble their efforts to excel and succeed can only make for greater productivity.

4. Latino investment income. Latinos receive very little income from interest, dividends, or rentals. Although this may be due in part to a lack of discretionary capital, the disturbing fact is that Latinos are simply not earning much investment income.

The most recent trends in labor and personnel relations build on the notion that if employees feel they have a stake in their employer's performance, they tend to be mindful of the employer's interests. We may think about this trend on a macro scale. It is important for all members of society to feel that they have a stake in the future. If some members feel they have no stake, they may not wish to participate in the solution of difficult policy questions, such as the support of the elderly. If large segments of the population feel disaffected and alienated, the very fabric of society may be torn apart.

From the perspective of investment, the Latino population has very little stake in the state. In 1985, barely 3.3 percent of total IDR income went to Latinos. To achieve parity with the Anglo population, they would have to receive nearly 10 times as much IDR income as they currently receive.

The disparity in investment may be seen as both a problem and an opportunity. The problem is as noted—that Latinos may feel they have very little stake in societal outcomes. The opportunity is this—that Latinos represent a large source of investment that has scarcely been tapped, and one that will of course hold even greater potential as their numbers grow.

Certainly, the overall investment picture would be quite a bit brighter were Latinos to invest at the same rate as Anglos. Under our high-achievement simulation, Latino income from investments would increase more than sixfold, from $8.9 billion to $55.3 billion. Increased investment within the state would be certain to stimulate great economic growth. To the extent that Latinos and other minorities are not encouraged to invest, California loses potential investment capital and productive opportunities.

Chapter Five

Education

Public education in California has fallen on hard times. During the 1950's and 1960's, under the influence of the Baby Boom, education was a high priority, and expansion was the order of the day. Both facilities and staffs were built up with generous financing, and the results seemed to bear out the wisdom of those expenditures.

Although per-capita spending for students rose over the 1978–81 period, it barely kept pace with inflation. As a result, by 1981 California was spending less on public education than most of the other states by every economic measure. In 1971 it ranked 19th in per-capita expenditures on students; by 1983 it had managed to drop to 45th (Stanford University 1984). Meanwhile, educational expenditures as a percentage of personal income decreased from 4.5 percent to 3.4 percent, a decrease that saw California's ranking drop to 49th.

In short, public education is a policy area suffering from neglect. And those who are bound to be hurt by that neglect are the Latino students, the fastest-growing segment of the school-age population. In this chapter we shall first look at disparities in educational achievement between Latinos and non-Latinos, then at differences between foreign-born and native-born Latinos, and finally at certain disturbing trends in higher education and in the teaching profession. We shall conclude by pointing to some policy areas that warrant further work.

The Historical Trend

The educational gap between Latinos and other groups in the state has a long history, indicating deep-seated problems that require ambitious solutions. One good measure of educational achievement is the average number of years of schooling completed by adults age 25 years and older. Overall this figure has steadily climbed in California. In 1940 the average Anglo had only 9.8 years of schooling. Comparatively few Californians had graduated from high school, and college was but a distant dream for most. By 1980, thanks to the massive expenditures put into education after the Second World War, the statewide education attainment average had climbed to 12.3 years. However, these expenditures did not succeed in closing the long-standing educational gap between Latinos and non-Latinos, particularly Anglos. In 1940 Latinos had about four years less schooling than the Anglos' average, 5.6 years. And though by 1980 this figure had risen to 9.0 years, the Anglo average had climbed to 12.9 years. For 40 years there has been a gap of about four years educational achievement between Latinos and Anglos (see Fig. 5.1).

A similarly persistent gap is seen in the rate of high school graduation. In 1940 38.4 percent of Anglos graduated from high school; in 1980 the figure was 79.4 percent. The Latino population had a dismal graduation rate of 9.0 percent in 1940; by 1980 the rate had increased to only 41.0 percent, about where the Anglos stood 40 years before (see Fig. 5.2).

As one would expect from these dropout rates, the differential is repeated at the level of higher education. In 1940 a college diploma was something of a rarity in California; only 7.2 percent of Anglos were college graduates. Among Latinos a four-year diploma was extremely rare: just 1.6 percent of Latinos were college graduates. Federal and state programs (such as the G.I. Bill and the development of the California state college system) raised the Anglo figures considerably, to 21.2 percent by 1980. But the Latinos' rate climbed only a little, to barely 5.4 percent (see Fig. 5.3). Postsecondary education for Latinos today is below comparable levels for Anglos in 1940.

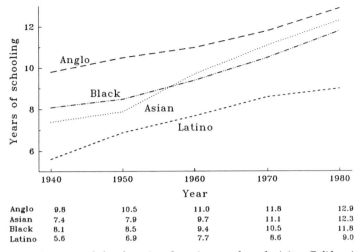

	1940	1950	1960	1970	1980
Anglo	9.8	10.5	11.0	11.8	12.9
Asian	7.4	7.9	9.7	11.1	12.3
Black	8.1	8.5	9.4	10.5	11.8
Latino	5.6	6.9	7.7	8.6	9.0

Fig. 5.1. Average adult educational attainment by ethnicity, California, 1940–1980. Source: Same as Fig. 4.1, pp. 13–15, 30. Figs. 5.2 and 5.3 are from the same source. In all three figures "Asian" equals "Asian and others."

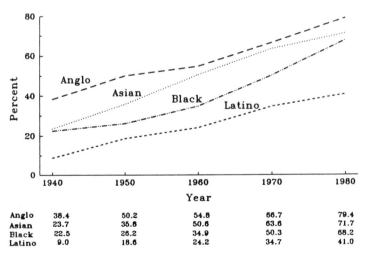

	1940	1950	1960	1970	1980
Anglo	38.4	50.2	54.8	66.7	79.4
Asian	23.7	35.8	50.6	63.6	71.7
Black	22.5	26.2	34.9	50.3	68.2
Latino	9.0	18.6	24.2	34.7	41.0

Fig. 5.2. Percent of adults completing high school by ethnicity, California, 1940–1980

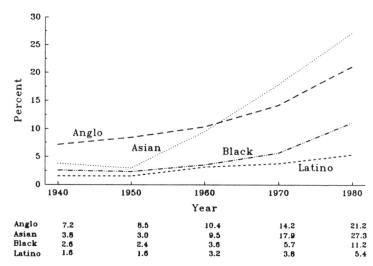

Anglo	7.2	8.5	10.4	14.2	21.2
Asian	3.8	3.0	9.5	17.9	27.3
Black	2.6	2.4	3.6	5.7	11.2
Latino	1.6	1.6	3.2	3.8	5.4

Fig. 5.3. Percent of adults completing college by ethnicity, California, 1940–1980

Current Achievement

By all the three measures above—average years of schooling, percentage of high school graduates, and percentage of college graduates—the Latino population in 1980 stood about where the Anglo population stood in 1940. Of all the major ethnic groups in the state, the Latinos have the dubious distinction of having the lowest educational achievement; only Native Americans, a much smaller group, are lower. Moreover, as was seen in Figure 5.1, the differences by ethnicity are significant. In terms of average educational achievement, both Anglos and Asians equaled or exceeded the statewide figure (12.3 years in 1980), with 12.9 and 12.3 years, respectively, and Blacks were close, at 11.8 years. Latinos, nearly 20 percent of the population, had 9.0 years.

These figures are alarming, not only for the Latino community, but also for the future of the public schools, in which Latino children represent a large and growing share of the new enrollments. In 1980, for example, they constituted over 30 percent of all the first-graders in the public schools (California, Assembly Office of

Research 1985). As shown in Figure 5.4, nearly every Latino child of elementary school age is attending school. However, the higher one looks, the greater the dropout rate, so that by age 17 more than a quarter of the Latino students have left.

What do we know about the quality of this education? The results of standardized tests are hardly reassuring. In 1984 the pass rate on the California Basic Educational Skills Test, administered to all high school seniors, was 76 percent for Anglos (Turner 1984: 26), only 40 percent for Latinos (and 36 percent for those of Mexican origin). Although Latinos are completing more years of school, those added years have not enabled them to compete on equal terms with non-Latinos.

Moreover, not all Latino groups have the same level of achievement. Nationwide, among the three main groups, Latinos of Mexican origin had the fewest years of schooling in 1980, 8.9 years, Puerto Ricans slightly more, 9.5, and Cubans the most, 11.5. In large part this gap is due to the fact that many of the Cubans who immigrated after the Revolution were fairly well-educated mem-

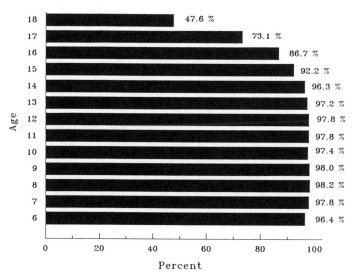

Fig. 5.4. Percent of Latinos enrolled in school by age, California, 1980. Source: Same as Fig. 2.6.

bers of the urban middle class, whereas the Mexican immigrants tend to be rural people with only minimal schooling. The Mexican Latino level, in consequence, tends to be dampened by the constant infusion of newcomers. In the 1980 census, in California, for example, adult Latinos over 25 years old born in Mexico reported having completed an average of only 7.1 years of school, but the figure for those born in the United States was 9.4, about the same level as the Puerto Rican group (USBC 1982b).

Because so many California Latinos are of Mexican origin, we might usefully take a quick look at the educational trends in Mexico.

Education in Mexico

Overall 64.3 percent of adults in Mexico have six years or more of schooling; thus 35.7 percent of all Mexicans have not even finished primary school. Literacy rates are perhaps more revealing than years of schooling, for the ability to read and write at some level may be attained after only a few years of education. In the following discussion, then, people with at least four years of schooling are considered literate.

Figure 5.5 charts the literacy rates in Mexico from 1940 to 1980. As we see, the literacy level rose substantially during that period. In 1940 more than half the country was illiterate, but by 1960 the figure had fallen to a third. And by 1970 the rate had been further reduced, to less than a quarter. What the national rates do not indicate, however, is the enormous difference between the urban and rural rates (see Fig. 5.5). As late as 1970 well over a third of the rural population was still illiterate, compared with only about 15 percent of urban dwellers. The implications of this rural-urban difference are immediately clear, for though the immigration figures are somewhat rough, as far as can be known the largest part of the Mexican immigrant stream has traditionally come from rural areas (in particular the states of Michoacan and Jalisco), that is to say, from those areas with the lowest educational achievement. As long as this rural-urban educational difference continues in Mexico and the bulk of the in-migrants who add to the Latino population in California are rural people, the overall educational achievement of the Mexican-origin population in California will be significantly affected.

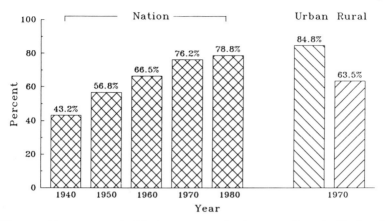

Fig. 5.5. Literacy rates in Mexico, 1940–1980. Sources: Consejo Nacional de Poblacion, *Mexico Demographico* (Mexico, D.F., 1978), p. 78; Ricardo Urioste, *Annuario Mexicano, 1982* (Mexico, D.F., 1982), pp. 72–73.

Effects on Labor Force

What does all this portend for the future work force? In 1980 working-age (16–64) Anglos had an educational level of 13.5 years, prime-age Latinos 10.4 years, and the total labor force 12.9 years. Under our baseline labor model, it will be recalled, Latinos will constitute 36.4 percent of the labor force by 2030. Assuming that the 1980 differentials are preserved, our calculations show that by 2030 the increased Latino representation would have the effect of lowering the overall educational achievement of the labor force to 12.1 years. That the labor force of 2030 would actually be less educated than in 1980 is bad enough; it would be particularly serious if, as seems certain, a more-educated, better-prepared labor force will be required for a high-tech future.

Under our immigration-influx scenario, in which there is a surge in immigration from Mexico for 10 years, the effect is predictably even more pronounced. The average educational level drops from 12.9 years in 1980 to 11.9 years in 2030, when Latinos would form 46.4 percent of the labor force.

Clearly, an increase in Latino educational achievement would serve the interests of the California economy. Unfortunately, current educational policies do not point in this direction, and the prognosis for a sharp improvement is not good.

Problems in Higher Education

In a future high-tech California economy, knowledge, rather than physical labor, will be the most valuable product. Indeed, that is already true to some extent today, with even agriculture, for example, being increasingly influenced by the use of computers, bioengineering, economic modeling, and the like; the generation of new knowledge is itself becoming the difference between economic vigor and economic stagnation (Gardner 1984). As Latinos and other minorities start to make up a larger portion of the state's population, their experiences with higher education cease to be a picturesque footnote and become, instead, a major focus for educational policy (Hodgkinson 1983).

Enrollment Gaps

If Latino educational achievement seems bad at the elementary and high school levels, it is positively dismal at the postsecondary level. Although only a rough indicator, one might reasonably expect to find Latinos substantially represented at all levels of higher education: in undergraduate and graduate enrollments, in all disciplines and majors, and on faculties and teaching staffs. Ideally, this would mean a proportionate representation of about 20 percent in each category. Let us see how far from ideal the actual situation is.

The logical place to begin is with the college-eligible pool—high school graduating seniors. Here the Latino students have mirrored a general trend of declining preparation for college study. In 1976 14.8 percent of all California seniors were eligible for the University of California system; by 1983 the figure had dropped to 13.2 percent. Similarly, in 1976 35 percent were eligible to study at one of the state colleges or universities, compared with only 29.2 percent in 1983.* Grade-point averages, enrollment in college-preparatory courses, and verbal and math scores on the Scholastic Aptitude Test all declined in this period (California Postsecondary Education Commission 1984).

*Hereafter in this discussion we use UC for the entire University of California system and CSU for the state college–state university system.

When we compare the performance of different ethnic groups, however, we find that the decline was most severe among Latinos. In 1983 only 4.9 percent of Latino students were eligible for UC, compared with 15.5 percent of Anglos; and only 15.3 percent were eligible for CSU, compared with 33.5 percent of Anglos.

Given this small pool of college-eligible Latinos, it is hardly surprising that they are badly underrepresented in higher education. In 1981 Latinos accounted for 5.4 percent of all UC undergraduates. This is an abysmally small proportion, not even close to the 20 percent ideal; and yet it is an improvement over the 1977 figure—4.9 percent. Latinos are slightly better represented in CSU, with 7.5 percent of undergraduate enrollments in 1981, an improvement from their 5.6 percent in 1977.

Distribution by Major

Equally disturbing is the Latinos' low share of enrollments in such important fields for the high-tech future as computer sciences and mathematics. As Table 5.1 shows, as late as 1981 Latinos tended to be skewed in the direction of the humanities and away from the sciences and mathematics, an unpromising trend in an era in which technology holds the key to the future. An encouraging sign is that the second- and third-most popular majors among Latinos were biological sciences and engineering, fields that have been targeted for recruiting and retention efforts.

Graduate Education

The picture of graduate-level education is worse still. It is in the laboratories, computer centers, seminar rooms, and libraries that tomorrow's knowledge is being developed and refined today. It is precisely at this level that the failure of the educational system to engage the Latino student is most marked. Again we shall concentrate on UC, which awards most of the doctorates in the state. In 1980–81 only 19 of the 2,111 UC doctoral degrees were awarded to Latino students—or just 0.9 percent of the total. Further, not one of these doctorates was earned in computer sciences or mathematics. Nine were in social sciences, four in engineering, three in biological sciences, two in psychology, and one each in education and the physical sciences (medical and law degree sciences are

88   *Education*

Fields of Study of Latino Undergraduates in the
University of California System, 1981

Discipline	Total enrollment	Latino enrollment	Latino as percent of total
Public affairs and services	159	13	13.2%
Foreign languages	835	109	13.0
Area studies	147	16	10.8
Psychology	2,466	167	6.7
Education	257	16	6.2
Social sciences	8,407	512	6.1
Architecture	664	40	6.0
Biological sciences	5,697	304	5.3
Communications	827	37	4.4
Letters	3,096	129	4.1
Business management	1,880	76	4.0
Fine arts	2,731	109	3.9
Engineering	5,011	182	3.6
Agriculture	1,330	45	3.3
Physical sciences	2,018	66	3.2
Mathematics	1,142	34	2.9
Computer science	1,331	31	2.3
Interdisciplinary and other	5,367	293	5.5
TOTAL	43,365	2,179	5.8%

SOURCE: California Postsecondary Education Commission, *Postsecondary Education in California, 1982 Information Digest* (Sacramento, 1984).

not included in these data; California Postsecondary Education Commission 1984). An even greater underutilization of potential talent is seen in the breakdown of doctoral degrees by sex. The total figures split 51.7 percent men, 48.3 percent women; but 17 of the 19 Latino doctorates, or fully 90 percent, were earned by men.

The one bright spot in this otherwise dismal picture is seen in the field of the health sciences, an area that has been specifically targeted for affirmative action. Since 1970 programs have been funded by public agencies and private foundations to encourage Latinos and other minorities to prepare for and study medicine, dentistry, nursing, pharmacology, and optometry. That effort appears to have paid off, at least to the extent that Latinos are better represented in the health sciences than in other areas of graduate studies. Although in 1981 Latinos earned less than 1 percent of all

UC doctorates, in the health sciences they received 6.6 percent of the medical or equivalent professional doctoral degrees. Broken down by health science specialty, Table 5.2 shows 10.2 percent for dentistry, 6.9 percent for medicine, 5.3 percent for optometry, and 3.4 percent for pharmacology. These are respectable gains over a decade that started with virtually no Latino providers.

Faculty

But the health sciences are only one of many areas in need of such efforts if the Latino population is to achieve educational parity. One obvious place to start is with the teaching staff. At present the Latino public elementary school pupil is not very likely to encounter a Latino teacher to serve as role model or instructor. In 1981 the overall teacher-student ratio in the state system was 1 : 24, and the Anglo-to-Anglo ratio was 1 : 17. The Latino figures, however, were very wide of the mark, with only one Latino teacher for every 104 Latino students (Turner 1984: 23). To be sure, there is no guarantee that a Latino teacher will teach Latino students better than a non-Latino teacher; indeed, some non-Latino teachers have developed extremely good teaching methods for their Latino students. Nevertheless, there are indications that Latinos on the teaching staff of a school with a predominantly Latino student body would bring benefits in the form of social and cultural sensitivity, positive role modeling, and greater community involvement.

But in order for this to happen, a shortfall in Latino teachers has to be made up. In 1979 there were 166,440 teachers in the

TABLE 5.2
Latino Degree Recipients in the Health Professions in the
University of California System, 1981

Category	Dentistry (D.D.S.)	Medicine (M.D.)	Optometry (D.O.)	Pharmacology (P.Ph.)
Total number of degrees	176	567	113	59
Number of Latino recipients	18	39	6	2
Latinos as a percent of total	10.2%	6.9%	5.3%	3.4%

SOURCE: Same as Table 5.1.

state's public schools, of whom 9,205 (5.5%) were Latinos. By the 20-percent criterion, this means a shortfall of 24,083 Latino teachers. Although this seems like a large order to fill, bear in mind the gains that were made in the health sciences in just a little over 10 years. Plainly there are lessons to be learned in recruiting, preparing, admitting, and retaining Latino students from that effort that could be applied to other disciplines.

From all that we have seen to this point, it can come as no surprise to find that Latino representation on the UC and CSU faculties is minimal: not quite 2.7 percent (315 of 11,823 in 1981) in the first case, 3.1 percent (365 of 11,709) in the second. A faculty member's area of research is a highly personal choice, usually built around some interest strong enough to sustain the person throughout the lean years of doctoral research and the harried years of full-time teaching and research, with the inevitable time spent on committees. For this reason, the question of specialty is an extremely sensitive area. We shall merely note that in the UC system Latino faculty are concentrated in a very few areas, generally the social sciences, literature, and ethnic studies. Because many of these professors tend to attract Latino graduate students, there is a multiplier effect, accounting in part for the skewed distribution of students across disciplines.

Policy Areas for Consideration

Most current policy has focused on the quantitative outcomes of educational achievement. These outcomes still require attention and effort, for they reflect a shrinking Latino presence as one moves up the educational ladder. We would like to suggest, however, some new policy areas for attention. In our experience Latino education has been approached as a problem of remediation, with most efforts aimed at low achievers and non-English speakers. Certainly, we would not deny that these efforts are needed, and in greater amounts than currently available, but we believe that policy needs to focus at the top of the achievement scale as well.

1. Critical masses of excellence. As a means of achieving the quantitative goals, we advocate a qualitative approach. To encour-

age Latino participation and achievement in education, we believe that intellectual "critical masses" of faculty and doctoral candidates need to be established at the university level—in particular, at the University of California campuses and selected private universities where research is emphasized. Each critical mass should be concentrated in a particular discipline, such as engineering, public health, computer science, or sociology. Ideally, each campus would have three or four such critical masses, consisting of focused, concentrated efforts in a delimited area. Through such networks of excellence, the potential of the Latino community might be tapped. Promising students at the undergraduate and high school levels could be identified and encouraged through these networks, and the excitement about new ideas could flow into the Latino community.

2. Latino educational personnel. Two areas of need can be identified in this connection. First, the number of Latino teachers must be increased at all levels. Second, at the postsecondary, professional, and graduate levels, the Latino faculties' disciplines must become more diversified. Specifically, there must be a push to increase Latino faculty in the sciences and in the professions.

3. Bilingual education. To this point we have avoided two touchy areas that must be discussed: bilingual education and the education of the undocumented. The first is a promise more honored in the breach than in the observance. We believe that a redefinition of bilingual education is called for. Currently, the aim is not to develop students so that they are equally proficient in English and their mother tongue, but to provide enough of a bridge that non-English speakers can learn other subjects while they are learning to master English. This is a very limited definition of bilingual education in our view. Given the present and future importance of the Pacific Rim market, true bilingualism at an advanced level should be made a priority. It would be in the state's interest to target a portion of students (say the top 20 percent) to be fully bilingual at the completion of high school in both English and some other Pacific Basin language—whether it be Spanish, Portuguese, Japanese, or a Chinese dialect (most likely Cantonese or Mandarin).

Currently, because of the limited definition of bilingual education, skills in languages other than English are neglected. Most Latino college students today cannot function at college level in Spanish in mathematics, let alone sociology, political theory, or computer programming. We contend that a substantial number of people must become fully functional in two languages if California is to capitalize on its position in the Pacific Rim economy.

4. Education of the undocumented. Undocumented immigrants, referred to by some legislators as the "undocumented taxpayers," have played, and will continue to play, a vital role in the state's economy; and the education of their children is an issue that will not go away, regardless of any immigration reform measure that might be passed. To exclude these children from quality education will serve only to harm the productivity of the future work force. Unfortunately, policy in the 1980's seems to be leaning in that direction. Certainly recent legislation requiring people without papers to pay full out-of-state tuition at public institutions will put higher education out of reach for most of them. This is a policy area that demands careful thought, with close attention paid to the consequences of denying education to a growing part of the state's population.

Chapter Six

Health Care

Health ranks with education as one of the two most important investments a society can make in itself. Investment in this area provides many payoffs. At the most elementary level, the provision of health services ensures the physical survival of a society. At more optimal levels, the attainment of a certain measure of good health and wellness enhances a society's quality of life and ability to function productively. Provision of basic health services to the children in the present ensures the existence of a healthy labor force in the future. And when the adult body ages and begins to lose some of its functional capacity, health-care services can alleviate suffering and compensate for some of the functional loss.

Although society's interest in the education of its members wanes after they are young adults, its interest in health care continues, and grows, as they become elderly. This need for health-care services all during a person's life span creates two separate policy challenges, linked ultimately through the intergenerational compact and the interethnic compact.

The first challenge is to make an investment decision across ethnic lines. An investment in the health of children is an investment in the future. Currently, nearly half of all children in California are minority, largely Latino. By 2030 only a third of all children will be Anglo. Clearly, the young Latino population represents a human resource that will require a health-care investment in the present in order to function well in the future. However, very little is known about their health-care needs, and health-care services traditionally have not served them well.

The second challenge is a payout decision across generational lines. The elderly require ever-increasing amounts of health-care services. Society's decision to assume a large portion of those costs is largely an ethical one, for the productivity gains achieved by such a massive expenditure are practically nil.

Currently, society has made the decision to assist the elderly with the cost of their health care: over half of all elderly health-care expenditures are paid for by public revenues (Kingson & Scheffler 1981). As the number of elderly increases, and as longevity increases, the provision of health-care services will become extremely expensive. At some point serious ethical discussion will be needed about the extent to which society will assume this burden. The field of critical care, in which extremely expensive procedures are used to prolong a person's life for a short time, demonstrates the coming ethical dilemma about the economics of life-and-death decisions (Mondragon 1985).

The health-care costs for the younger are much lower, and the productivity gains may be easily seen over the span of a person's life. A dollar invested in a person's health at age five will produce many dollars of benefits to society for many decades. Unlike the elderly, the young have to turn to the family rather than public programs for health-care expenditures.

Seemingly, the resource allocation decision would be simple: society should invest in the relatively inexpensive preventive measures for the health of children, so that they will be physically able to shoulder the swollen costs for the elderly in the future. The problem is that a seemingly simple generational issue is compounded by the ethnic issue: increasingly, the children of the state are Latino and other minority, while the elderly will be largely Anglo. As we have seen in the areas of employment and education, Latinos do not obtain the same level of benefit as the rest of the population. We suspect that the same holds true for health care; worse, once an issue is deemed to be a "Latino issue," it tends not to receive adequate attention and resources. In the case of health care, there is the additional tug of the almost implacable need of the elderly for the health resources of society.

In the future the Latino and minority younger generation will have to compete with the largely Anglo elderly for health-care resources. The ethical question of who will live and who will not will be discussed in highly political arenas, as programs and policies are debated and developed.

The input to these debates is uneven. Much is known about Anglo health and elderly health: projections about their future needs have been made often, and with great confidence. Very little is known about Latino health needs, and projections about specific needs cannot be made with any great degree of confidence: after all, if the current need is not known, how can future need be projected? In order to provide some sense of future health-care policy debates, we present here some basic frameworks for viewing Latino health. The major processes that affect Latino health are developed along with some data about their influence currently.

Health and Society

The health of a population is never static; it is constantly changing. New policies and programs must therefore be continually developed. Industrialization and urbanization, for instance, bring a set of quite different illnesses from those of a preindustrial society, requiring many new kinds of services and treatment. By and large preindustrial societies are characterized by communicable diseases: many people die, at all ages, of various epidemics that sweep through the population on a fairly regular basis. Once the society becomes more and more developed, the causes of death begin to change, and the death rates drop.

The United States made this transition in the nineteenth century. National data of the preindustrial period are hard to come by, but city samples can serve to tell the tale. Table 6.1 shows the principal causes of death in Philadelphia and Chicago in the 1860's and 1870's. In the years 1868–72 about 320 of every 100,000 Philadelphians died each year of pulmonary tuberculosis. That disease, like the others shown (diarrhea, pneumonia, smallpox, and typhoid fever), is transmitted from one person to another and is a disease of underdevelopment, the result of poverty, overcrowding, poor nutrition, and poor sanitation. Although the Chicago death rates in that period were lower, the same diseases, in almost identical order, were the major scourges there.

With the onset of industrialization (and before the advent of modern drugs, which were not in wide use until the Second World War), communicable diseases were nearly eradicated in the

TABLE 6.1

Principal Causes of Death, Philadelphia and Chicago, 1860's–1870's

(Deaths per 100,000 population per year)

Philadelphia (1868–72)		Chicago (1868–73)	
Cause	Annual rate	Cause	Annual rate
Pulmonary tuberculosis	320.7	Pulmonary tuberculosis	182.8
Diarrhea and enteritis	235.4	Diarrhea and enteritis	160.9
Pneumonia	153.0	Pneumonia	133.4
Smallpox	132.5	Typhoid fever	98.3
Typhoid fever	64.0	Smallpox	87.7

SOURCE: Winslow et al., *The History of American Epidemiology* (St. Louis, Mo., 1952), pp. 53, 59.

TABLE 6.2

Principal Causes of Death, United States, 1979

(Deaths per 100,000 population)

Cause	Rate
Heart disease	333.1
Malignant neoplasm (cancer)	183.3
Cerebrovascular disease	97.0
Accidents, violence	47.8
Chronic obstructive pulmonary disease	22.7

SOURCE: National Center for Health Statistics, *Vital Statistics of the United States, 1979* (Washington, D.C., 1984), p. 6.

United States, and the death rate dropped sharply. Economic development and elementary public-health measures were largely responsible for the eradication of the communicable diseases. Because of the rise in standards of living, by 1979 the principal causes of death were very different from those of the nineteenth century. None of the diseases shown in Table 6.2 (heart disease, malignant neoplasms, cerebrovascular disease, and accidents) are communicable, and none are associated with poor sanitation or poverty. Rather, these are the diseases of an advanced industrial society, arising in a style of living and in exposure to elements and risks that were unknown earlier.

In many ways Mexico and the United States offer stark contrasts to each other. Not only do they represent a pediatric population next to an increasingly geriatric one; they also represent one economy that has only recently begun the development and urbanization process next to another that has reached a mature level of development and is moving into the postindustrial stage. As we shall see shortly, Mexico tends to suffer from the diseases of underdevelopment, while the United States suffers from those of development. These two different epidemiological profiles converge in the Latino population in California.

Latino Health Variables

Unfortunately, so little is known about Latino health needs and services utilization that this epidemiological convergence cannot be measured, and projections for specific health needs cannot be made.

We present a conceptual model that will help sensitize us to some of the major health-care needs by emphasizing the fact that the Latino population is extremely heterogeneous. The major variable that subdivides this population is immigration, which we posit affects the health profile. Consider this example of two adult Latinos. One is a recently arrived Mexican from the rural state of Michoacan, and the other is a native-born Californian, living in urban Los Angeles. The first Latino was born and raised in a region with little development and has suffered the illnesses of that environment. His growth and development as a child, the communicable diseases to which he was exposed, his dental health— all were products of his health environment that contributed to the health profile he possesses in California. The California-born Latino was exposed to a different health environment, grew and developed differently, perhaps had better access to services, and consequently will present a different health profile. These two will respond differently to the same working and living conditions, and will have access to different systems of care, more likely than not. Immigration affects their health in the following manner.

Nativity. The Mexican-origin Latino population was 37 percent foreign-born in 1980 (USBC 1982b). Given the massive immigration since then, we posit that now close to half of California's

Mexican-origin population was born abroad. The health of Mexico will influence the health of Latinos in California.

Permanence. Of those born in Mexico, some reside in California permanently and others non-permanently. The non-permanents, also called seasonal immigrants, spend part of the year in the California health environment and part in the Mexican environment. We do not know the relative size of the permanent and seasonal populations, but we can appreciate that their differential exposures affect the California health profile.

Documentation. Of those born in Mexico, some enjoy documented status and others do not. Obviously, those who are undocumented find barriers to health-care services and program participation. We do not know the relative size of the documented and undocumented population or all of the effects of undocumentation on health. Further, there are families, termed binational families (Chavez 1983), in which some members are documented and others not. We do not know the size of this subpopulation or the effect of binationality.

In our perspective the Latino population has to be seen as very heterogeneous, with subpopulations (as defined by nativity, permanence, and documentation) enjoying different levels of health and differential access to services. Given that so little is known of these subpopulations, including their size, we do not offer specific health-needs projections for Latinos. Rather, we offer some information and data about the relation between society and health that will give a rough picture of areas of policy concern in future.

Latino Health Overview

Through experience with health-services utilization research on the Latino population in California, we have come to the tentative conclusion that native-born Latinos present a health profile approaching that of the rest of the state's population, while the foreign-born present a profile that approaches Mexico's. If combined, the entire Latino population would present a health profile somewhere between California's and Mexico's. Because the population projections are sensitive to immigration, we feel it best to provide some insight on how the foreign-born population might influence future health needs, even though we do not know much about its health needs currently. Assuming that this foreign-born portion resembles the Mexican health profile, we offer data on one of the major sending states in Mexico, Jalisco, to provide a baseline for policy speculation.

Health in Jalisco

Examining the health picture of the state of Jalisco serves our purposes splendidly, not only because it is a major sending area of immigrants to California, but also because it is an area now making the transition from preindustrial to industrial, a fact that is reflected in the changes in its health profile between 1940 and 1980 (see Table 6.3). In 1940 Jalisco was little industrialized, with 59.8 percent of the population still living in rural areas. Mortality data for that year are indicative of an underdeveloped region: communicable diseases were the principal causes of death, and death rates were quite high. In the course of the next 40 years, Jalisco became a largely urban state (in 1978 only 33.4 percent of its 4.2 million residents lived in rural areas), with a fair degree of industrialization. Its 1980 health profile reflects that shift. Not only did the death rates fall dramatically between 1940 and 1980, but two (mostly) urban ills, accidents and homicides, replaced the communicable disease of diarrhea as the leading cause of death. Communicable diseases are still prevalent, however, as the 1982

TABLE 6.3
Principal Causes of Death, Jalisco, 1940 and 1980
(Deaths per 100,000 population)

1940		1980	
Cause	Rate	Cause	Rate
Diarrhea	653.5	Accidents and homicides	93.3
Pneumonia	315.2	Influenza and pneumonia	63.1
Measles	74.5	Diarrhea and enteritis	62.1
Accidents and homicides	72.6	Malignant tumors	50.2
Typhoid fever	47.9	Perinatal mortality	40.0

SOURCE: Instituto Mexicano de Seguro Social, *Jalisco: Diagnostico de Salud* (Guadalajara, 1984), pp. 2.5, 2.9.

TABLE 6.4
Incidence of Communicable Disease, Jalisco, 1982
(Cases per 100,000 population)

Disease	Number of cases	Disease	Number of cases
Acute respiratory		Pneumonia	129
infection	15,607	Paratyphoid	128
Diarrhea	7,400	Strep throat	53
Intestinal parasites	1,512	Viral hepatitis	34
Influenza	789	Scabies	28
Chickenpox	229		

SOURCE: Same as Table 6.3, p. 31.

TABLE 6.5
Principal Causes of Death of Anglos and Mexican-Origin Latinos,
California, 1980
(Rank order)

Anglo	Mexican Latino
Heart disease	Heart disease
Malignant neoplasm	Accidents
Cerebrovascular disease	Malignant neoplasm
Accidents	Homicides
Chronic obstructive pulmo-	Cerebrovascular disease
nary disease	Perinatal conditions
Pneumonia and influenza	Cirrhosis and liver disease
Chronic liver disease	Congenital anomalies
Suicides	Pneumonia and influenza
Atherosclerosis	Diabetes mellitus
Homicides	

SOURCE: California Department of Health Services, Center for Health Statistics, *Data Matters* (Sacramento, Sept. 1982), p. 25.

TABLE 6.6
Death Rates of Anglos and Latinos by Age,
California, 1980
(Deaths per 100,000 in age group)

Age group	Anglo	Latino
1–24	80.6	72.5
25–44	163.4	158.4
45–64	902.4	607.6
65 & up	5,195.7	3,615.2

SOURCE: California Department of Health Services, Center for Health Statistics, *Public Health Dataline* (Sacramento, 1984), p. 4.
NOTE: Latino rates reported here are known to understate actual rates because of the imprecision of the ethnic identifier on death certificates in 1980.

rates shown in Table 6.4 indicate. In sum, the state's health profile shows a mixture of communicable diseases (influenza and diarrhea) and style-of-life diseases (accidents, malignancies), as one would expect in a society moving from preindustrial to industrial, together with a high rate of perinatal mortality (deaths occurring during pregnancy and childbirth), as one would expect in a young, fertile population.

Health in California

California data on the level of health of the Latino population are sketchy (Aranda 1971). But death certificates provide a few clues. The data for 1980, given in Table 6.5, show some differences in the 10 leading causes of death among Anglos and Latinos. Two of the differences observed among the Latinos probably reflect the influence of occupation and social class (the relatively high incidence of accidents and homicides) and two others the large proportion of women of childbearing age in this population (perinatal mortality and congenital anomalies).

One particular intriguing pattern is suggested by Table 6.6. In 1980 the Latinos had lower death rates, at all ages, than Anglos— in fact they had the lowest of any ethnic group in the state. There is some speculation that this unexpected pattern may be due to underreporting, and possibly also to people returning to Mexico to die. Whatever its cause, the same pattern has been found in Texas (Fonner 1975).

There are no statewide data on Latino morbidity, apart from a very few reportable communicable diseases. Small area studies provide the fullest data we have, but they should be generalized only with great caution. In any case, the fact that so many problems of identification, response, and questionnaire administration have recently turned up in connection with the sampling of Latino communities counsels caution in accepting the findings.

One disease for which reliable data *are* available is cancer, and here the Latino rates are generally lower than average. Menck et al. (1975), in a Los Angeles study, found that adult male Mexican immigrants and native-born males and females had lower rates of cancer in all its forms than other city residents. In many cases— malignant melanomas, lymphomas, and cancers of the mouth, bladder, larynx, and lungs—the Latinos' rates appear to be well below those of other groups (Stern et al. 1975). In others—cancers of the stomach, gallbladder, liver, nose, male genitals, and connective tissue—there is some evidence that Latinos are at more risk than other groups, but the differences are slight and have been shown for only a small geographic area.

One form of cancer in which the Latino population is clearly at much higher risk is cervical cancer. In Los Angeles, for example, the Latinas' rate of cervical cancer is more than twice as high as the Anglos' (22.9 cases per 100,000 women vs. 10.2; Waterhouse et al. 1982). This finding is consistent with a pattern found all over Latin America, where the rates range as high as 52.9 cases per 100,000 women in Colombia and 37.5 in Brazil. Whether this phenomenon is due to the high number of births among Latinas (Menck et al. 1975) or the sexual behavior of their partners (Zunzunegui et al. 1985), or both (or neither), cervical cancer is the one area in which Latinos differ sharply from non-Latinos.

The incidence of most other health problems among Latinos cannot even be guessed at. A survey conducted by the Alameda County (California) Human Population Laboratory (Roberts & Lee 1980) suggests that Latinos are much less likely to report health problems than either Anglos or Blacks. Latinos reported fewer instances of disability, fewer chronic conditions, and fewer symptoms than the general population.

Since there are important differences in income and education between native-born and foreign-born Latinos, we may assume there are differences in epidemiology as well. The health profile of the foreign-born is probably something like the sending country's, the native-born's closer to that of the United States. Therefore, in the long run we would expect shifts not only in the sending country's profile as it becomes more industrialized, but also in the U.S. Latinos' profile as new generations born in this country draw closer to the national average in income and education.

Health-Needs Projections

Health care is an area that is certain to be most directly affected by the age-skewing of the U.S. population. The health needs of the elderly can be foreseen with a fair degree of certainty. To a limited extent the same may be said of the younger population. A population that has a large number of women of childbearing age, for example, will predictably require services in prenatal care, delivery care, maternal care, and child growth and development care. Since the younger population in the early twenty-first century will be a heavily Latino population, the one uncertainty is the degree to which that population may vary from U.S. norms. As we have seen above, so far as the Latino population is concerned, the degree of variance is simply not known.

The general policy concern we project is that health problems will tend to become perceived as ethnic-related. That is, because of the preponderance of Anglos in the older cohorts, health problems of the elderly might easily become perceived as being Anglo problems; and, conversely, because of the preponderance of Latinos in the younger cohorts, problems of maternal health and child growth and development might become perceived as being Latino problems.

We should like to stress that for future health policy and planning, the separate effects of age and ethnicity need to be held apart, so that the influence of each may be taken into account.

The Health Needs of the Elderly

The health needs of the elderly have been frequently projected, and a brief summary is all that is needed here. As longevity increases, as it seems certain to do, some increases in chronic and degenerative diseases are to be expected (Gruenberg 1977; Manton 1982). These may be accompanied, in the view of some, by a "pandemic" of mental disorders (Kramer 1980). All of this translates into the need for increased services. In the following discussion, we shall single out the most important of the services, relying on the projections of Rice & Feldman (1982) for the period 1980–2040.

The ADL profile (activities of daily living) measures a person's ability to function in the daily course of living, including such activities as getting in and out of bed, using a toilet, dressing, and walking. In 1980 an estimated 3.1 million Americans needed assistance in performing at least one such activity. By the year 2040 that number will more than double, to 7.9 million. This assistance, if not available from a family member, has to be supplied by a professional care giver.

Hospitals, more than any other form of health-care services, will be most affected by the increase in elderly. Nationally, in 1980 the elderly accounted for 89.9 million short-stay hospital days out of a total of 264 million, or nearly 34 percent. By 2040 they will need 269.3 million days, or 52 percent of the national total of 508.3 million.

Since nursing-home care is almost entirely age-related, there will be a very substantial increase in demand in this area. By 2040 the 1.3 million elderly in nursing homes in 1980 will have grown to 5.0 million, a nearly fourfold increase.

All these increases in demand for care will come at a heavy price. Expenditures on hospital care for the elderly, which accounted for 29.0 percent of the national total in 1980 ($64.5 billion of $219.0 billion), may easily account for 45.5 percent by 2040 ($167.5 billion of $369.0 billion). And nursing-home expenditures are expected to increase from $20.6 billion to $48.3 billion. These costs obviously form a large part of the burden of support that the younger generation will have to pick up.

The Health Needs of the Latinos

Because so little is known about the health status and health care of Latinos, it is impossible to make reliable projections about the use of services in the future. However, health planners, policy makers, and administrators need to consider certain characteristics of the Latino population in formulating long-range programs for health services: age, culture, class standing, nativity, permanence, and documentation.

We would not wish to predict how these characteristics will come together in the Latino population's needs of the future. In the following pages, therefore, we shall work with our age projections alone to suggest the likely magnitude of the future health-care needs of a young Latino population. For each age group from infancy to young adulthood and for women of childbearing age as a separate group, we shall give the projected representation in the year 2030 and then compare current Jalisco and California data

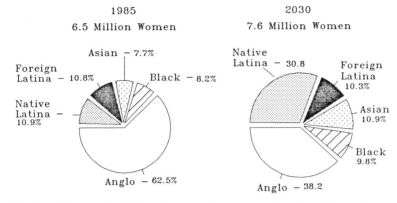

Fig. 6.1. Women of childbearing age (15–44) by ethnicity, California, 1985 and 2030, baseline assumptions

on the principal causes of death in order to identify the areas of likely need.

Women of childbearing age. Reproductive health is likely to be increasingly seen as a Latino problem as the proportion of Latinas among women of childbearing age grows. In 1985 only 21.7 percent of women 15–44 were Latinas, but by 2030 their share will be at least 41.1 percent (see Fig. 6.1). Within this group the major variable is the proportion of foreign-born. Fertility is higher among the foreign-born, and they are less likely to have had adequate nutrition, sanitation, and general health care as children. As a result they could be expected to have more reproductive problems than the native-born, and many of those problems are likely to go undetected until late into a pregnancy.

In California there were only 45 maternal deaths in 1980 resulting from complications of pregnancy and childbirth per 100,000 live births (CDHS 1984b: 49). Jalisco experienced 60.1 maternal deaths per 100,000 live births in 1978. Table 6.7 gives a breakdown of the principal causes of maternal death in Jalisco. A look at these causes points to the direction of future emphasis. Many of these deaths, as we see (54 percent of those shown in the table), can be attributed to a simple lack of medical attention during the birthing process, resulting in hemorrhaging, toxemia, and septic births. This is plainly one area of policy emphasis.

TABLE 6.7
Principal Causes of Maternal Death, Jalisco, 1978
(Deaths per 100,000 live births)

Cause	Rate
Complications of pregnancy, childbirth, and postpartum	25.0
Hemorrhaging	13.1
Toxemia	12.5
Sepsis	6.5
Abortion complications	3.0

SOURCE: Same as Table 6.3, p. 2.21.

TABLE 6.8
Principal Causes of Infant Death, California, 1980, and Jalisco, 1978
(Deaths per 1,000 live births)

California		Jalisco	
Cause	Rate	Cause	Rate
Perinatal conditions	5.9	Enteritis and diarrhea	10.4
Congenital anomalies	2.8	Pneumonia and influenza	8.8
Sudden infant death syndrome	2.1	Perinatal conditions	7.4
Accidents	0.3	Congenital anomalies	1.8
Pneumonia and influenza	0.2	Acute respiratory disease	1.2

SOURCES: California Department of Health Services, Center for Health Statistics, *Data Matters and Topical Reports* (Sacramento, 1983), p. 9; Instituto Mexicano de Seguro Social, *Jalisco: Diagnostico de Salud* (Guadalajara, 1984), p. 2.15.

TABLE 6.9
Principal Causes of Early Childhood (Ages 1–4) Death,
California, 1980, and Jalisco, 1978
(Deaths per 100,000 in age group)

California		Jalisco	
Cause	Rate	Cause	Rate
Accidents	35.0	Diarrhea and enteritis	70.4
Congenital anomalies	9.2	Accidents	68.4
Cancer	5.0	Pneumonia and influenza	48.7
Homicides	3.4	Nutritional deficiency	9.7
Pneumonia and influenza	1.6	Acute respiratory disease	8.5

SOURCES: California Department of Health Services, Center for Health Statistics, *Data Matters and Topical Reports* (Sacramento, 1983), p. 10; Instituto Mexicano de Seguro Social, *Jalisco: Diagnostico de Salud* (Guadalajara, 1984), p. 2.17.

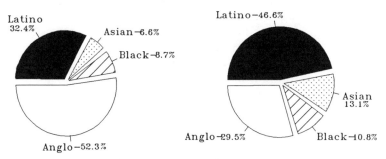

Fig. 6.2. Children ages 0–4 years by ethnicity, California, 1985 and 2030, baseline assumptions

There is another area where work should start at once: the possible effects of long-term exposure to mutagens and carcinogens must be tracked among Latinas as time passes. Both residential and working patterns place these women at risk to exposure to toxic substances.

Births. Under our baseline assumptions the proportion of Latino births will increase from 29.2 percent of all live births in 1981 (CDHS 1983b: 35) to 51.0 percent by 2030.

Table 6.8 shows the principal causes of infant death in California in 1980 and Jalisco in 1978, along with the rates of death. As may be seen, the greatest number of deaths in Mexico are from the diseases of underdevelopment: diarrhea, enteritis, influenza, and pneumonia.

Early childhood (ages 0–4). In 1985 Latino children accounted for 32.4 percent of all children ages 0–4. By our projections they will account for 46.6 percent in 2030 (see Fig. 6.2).

The childhood mortality rates for California and Jalisco are given in Table 6.9. The two profiles are strikingly different. Diarrhea and enteritis are negligible risks in California, but the most prevalent causes of early-childhood death in Jalisco; Jalisco's accident rate is over twice as high as California's; and although the death rate resulting from nutritional deficiencies is relatively low in Jalisco, this cause does not appear at all on the California list.

These rates quite plainly reflect the differences in development between Mexico and the United States. The Mexican health profile continues to show the characteristics of a preindustrial society. For children in this age group, then, it is critical that health education and prevention programs be designed so as to be accessible to large numbers of non-English-speaking parents. Moreover, because many early-childhood health conditions are correlates of the parents' education and income, it is not sufficient to think only in terms of programs that affect an individual child. Long-range programs aimed at increasing the parents' incomes and education might well be as important as immunization campaigns.

Late childhood (ages 5–14). In Table 6.10 we continue to note differences between the chief causes of death in Jalisco and California, with Jalisco children in the 5–14 age group, unlike those in California, still dying mainly from communicable diseases (diarrhea, enteritis, influenza, pneumonia, tuberculosis). The death rate from accidents is now nearly three times as high in Jalisco as in California. But the death rates overall are comparatively low in this age group, both in Mexico and in the United States. Basically, once a child has survived its first few years, the risk of early death is considerably reduced.

By the year 2030 Latinos will compose 46.0 percent of the 5–14 age group, up from 27.3 percent in 1985. For children in this age group the health needs are as likely to be social and psychological as physiological. Mental health problems become increasingly important; and with the onset of puberty the whole gamut of reproductive health problems comes into play. Because all these problems tend to be sensitive to the social and cultural climate, programs and services aimed at these children will have to be designed to handle the complexities of a Latino society and culture that are only barely discerned now, much less understood.

Early adulthood (ages 15–24). Adolescence and young adulthood are a time of life when mortality spikes upward. The bulk of these deaths, as is clear in Table 6.11, have social causes. This is particularly true of adolescents, a group in which approximately eight of ten deaths in California are not related to a medical condition. Mortality data for Jalisco are not available for this age group. However, judging from the state-wide figures, the accident and homicide rates were quite high in 1978. Peer groups, society in

TABLE 6.10

Principal Causes of Late Childhood (Ages 5–14) Death, California, 1980, and Jalisco, 1978

(Deaths per 100,000 in age group)

California		Jalisco	
Cause	Rate	Cause	Rate
Accidents	16.3	Accidents	44.2
Cancer	6.6	Pneumonia and influenza	5.6
Homicide	1.9	Diarrhea and enteritis	5.1
Congenital anomalies	1.9	Cancer	4.9
Heart disease	0.8	Tuberculosis	1.5

SOURCES: California Department of Health Services, Center for Health Statistics, *Data Matters and Topical Reports* (Sacramento, 1983), p. 11; Instituto Mexicano de Seguro Social, *Jalisco: Diagnostico de Salud* (Guadalajara, 1984), p. 2.19.

TABLE 6.11

Principal Causes of Early Adult (Ages 15–24) Death, California, 1980

(Deaths per 100,000 in age group)

Cause	Rate
Accidents	81.3
Homicides	33.7
Suicides	14.0
Cancer	6.4
Congenital anomalies	2.2

SOURCE: California Department of Health Services, Center for Health Statistics, *Data Matters and Topical Reports* (Sacramento, 1983), p. 12.

general, and working conditions influence this age group greatly. The ability of educational and prevention programs to link with the growing Latino population of this age bracket is the key to reducing mortality and morbidity.

From the projections above, it is clear that as Latinos grow in number, they will affect the younger generations disproportionately. Figure 6.3 shows the changing composition of the 0–15 age group in California from 1985 to 2030. As we see, Latino children will provide whatever growth there is in this group over the period and will become the plurality in about 2010. If current trends in the provision of health care continue, the

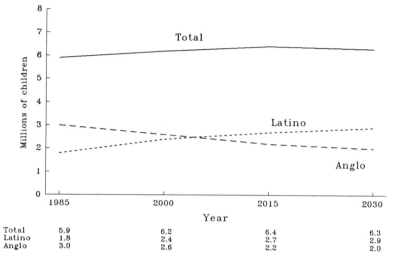

Fig. 6.3. Size of total, Anglo, and Latino populations ages 0–15 years, California, 1985–2030, baseline assumptions

care of these children will depend to a very large extent on their parents' ability to pay for it, people who will at the same time be expected to contribute to the public programs that will carry the elderly in their time of medical need.

For all the age brackets, there are mental health issues to be taken into account. The effects of immigration on the mental health of Latinos are scarcely explored, but one can easily guess that the strains of moving from a rural to urban environment, one where family structure, sex roles, and personal identity are different, will have a deleterious effect. Alcoholism, drug use, petty crime, gangs and gang warfare, family breakup, and spouse and child abuse are possible negative mental health outcomes, but they have been so inadequately researched in the Latino community that little definitive can be said about them. We can only mention that they exist.

Professional Manpower Needs

Professional manpower is a related area in which some policy work needs to be done. Though there is no direct proof that the future health needs of the Latino population could be met by the

simple expedient of increasing the number of Latino professionals, there is some evidence that Latinos and other minority
professionals tend to establish their practices within their ethnic
groups (Montoya et al. 1978). The fact of ethnicity alone of course
does not guarantee that a professional would be proficient in another language, or that he or she would be any more or less empa-
thetic to the community. However, in a society in which there
were no barriers to full participation, one could reasonably expect
that Latinos would be randomly and evenly distributed in all occupations, so that there should be some sort of representative
proportion of Latinos among the health professionals.

As things currently stand, Latinos are extremely underrepresented in all the professions. This may be seen quite clearly in
the case of the health professions: in 1980 only 973 or 1.8 percent,
of the 54,082 licensed physicians in California and only 549, or
3.6 percent, of the dentists were Latino. Nurses fared only slightly
better. Of 130,168 licensed R.N.s, only 7,336, or 5.6 percent, were
Latino (California Office of Statewide Health Planning and Development 1982).

The acute shortage of Latino providers is seen most clearly in
Figure 6.4, showing provider-to-population data for physicians

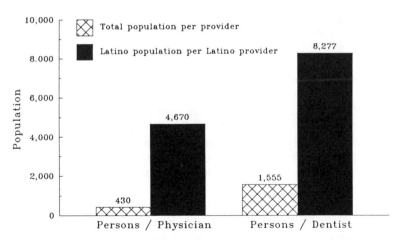

Fig. 6.4. Population per provider, physicians and dentists, California,
1980. Source: California Office of Statewide Health Planning and Development, *EEO Special File* (Sacramento, 1982).

and dentists in California. The ratio for physicians in general in 1980 was one to every 430 people. But in the Latino community, the ratio was nearly 11 times lower—1 : 4,670. Similarly, for Latino dentists, the ratio was about a fifth of the state ratio. Health providers often serve as a voice in health-care policy discussions. The lack of Latino providers will hamper the Latino attempts at obtaining a voice in the health-policy debates that will arise as we move toward an age-ethnic stratified society.

Age, Ethnicity, and Health Policy

A generational competition for health-care resources may be developing. This beginning competition is most noticeable when examining the current and future trends in health-care costs for the different generations.

The rapid increase in health costs has been a major policy concern for the past 20 years. In 1970 total national health-care expenditures were $74.9 billion (USBC 1986a: 97). By 1980 this figure had climbed to $387.4 billion. The 516 percent increase between the two figures is far greater than the rate of inflation over the same period. In 1984 the rate of increase in health-care expenditures was 9.1 percent per year, still much higher than the rate of inflation.

In 1970 the annual per-capita expenditure for health services for the elderly was $428, compared with only $198 for the population age 64 and under. For children ages 0–5 the expenditure was even lower—$105 per child per year (Rudov & Santangelo 1979: 265). The elderly expenditures were over twice those for the rest of the population, and four times the amount for children.

By 1980 the per-capita expenditure for the elderly had increased to $1,760 per year; and for the rest of the population it had increased to nearly three and one-half times that of the younger generations (U.S. Health Resources and Services Administration 1985: 260).

Increasingly since 1960, the elderly have turned to public programs to assist in obtaining health services. To date nearly half of these expenditures was paid for by public funds (Kingson & Scheffler 1981), and an additional 30 percent was paid by insurance. By contrast, children have done less well (Preston 1984).

The number of children enrolled nationally under Medicaid coverage declined from 10.5 million in 1979 to 8 million in 1982 (Davis 1983).

Clearly, a generational conflict is under way, with children likely to have fewer resources available to them in the future than they do now, and the elderly likely to have more. And Latino children, we opine, are likely to find themselves in a worse position. Nationally, Latinos are able to expend only 79 percent as much on health care as the rest of the under-64 population, are much less likely to see a physician, and are much less likely to be hospitalized (Guendelman & Schwalbe 1986). This low rate of participation will intensify the generational competition. Once again, we see the intergenerational relation turning, in California and other areas with large Latino populations, into an interethnic competition.

Decisions about a possible rationing of health-care resources have to be made in the future. These decisions are, ultimately, ethical and moral ones as well as economic ones. How will the decision be made that the elderly receive too many of the health-care resources? How will the decision be made to finance their heavy utilization? How does society decide who is to live, and who to die? How do Latinos participate in these discussions, when so little is known about their health-care needs?

Policy Areas for Consideration

1. Latino health statistics. It is virtually impossible to develop reasonable policy in the absence of basic indicators of health status and utilization. Only recently have a few agencies begun including Latino identifiers on reporting forms. Such data need to be uniformly and routinely collected on a state and national basis. Furthermore, statistical sampling procedures must ensure representative sampling of Latinos, including the difficult-to-reach undocumented.

2. Health-services needs. Effort needs to be refocused on maternal and child health care, with special emphasis on the unique Latino needs in this domain. Programs for the delivery of prenatal care, birth care, and infant, early childhood, and adolescent care should be developed that take into account the variables that

make Latino health status and utilization different from the norm: age, class standing, immigration, and culture. Programs developed for an Anglo, middle-class clientele might not be accessible to most of the Latino population.

3. Mental health. Status as a Latino in an Anglo-oriented culture brings about strains that can lead to mental health problems. The effects of immigration—changes in culture (both Mexican to American and rural to urban), in sex roles, and in family structure, and the uncertainty of national identity—operate to create unique mental health problems in the Latino community.

4. Health manpower. There is a tremendous shortfall in the numbers of Latino physicians, dentists, and nurses relative to the size of the Latino population. Apart from the obvious need to increase Latino enrollments in professional schools, consideration should be given to two short-term measures: recruiting doctors from the huge surplus in Mexico and training non-Latinos specifically for work in the Latino community.

5. Health in Mexico. Health knows no borders. Health efforts in Mexico necessarily have a considerable effect on the health of California Latinos. There is a need for greater cooperative work in health between the United States and Mexico. Comprehensive programs of joint research, policy development, implementation, and evaluation need to be set in motion.

Chapter Seven

Political Participation

Many of the policy decisions to be made on how the elderly are to be supported, by whom, and out of what funds are basically political questions, questions that will be considered—and ultimately answered—via the political process. Two groups in particular will have a great deal at stake in the outcome of such decisions: the elderly and the young Latinos. Our analysis leads us to believe that the two groups will not be participating in the decision-making processes equally. Following the framework presented by Hirschman in his classic work *Exit, Voice and Loyalty*, we see that voice is an important and desirable form of participation. Currently, the Anglo population has a prominent voice in such deliberations, while the Latino voice is so soft as to be almost unheard. This disparity in voice will pose grave problems as we move toward an age-ethnic stratified society. In this chapter we shall illustrate the compositional effects of the Latino population that tend to dampen its voice.

Measuring Voice

We may construct a "voice ratio" that gives an index of the relative strength of a group's voice. It shows for every 1,000 registered voters the number of unregistered people whose concerns must be carried by those who participate. If a group has few participants and large numbers of nonparticipants, its voice will be low: there are very few attempting to express the political concerns of the many. Conversely, a group with many participants and few nonparticipants will have a high voice: the concerns of most may be expressed directly.

Nonparticipation is due to many factors: age, citizenship, registration, income, and education. We shall examine each one in more detail shortly. For now, we may construct the voice ratio using our state figures on age structure and citizenship and national figures on age structure and citizenship and national figures (USBC 1983a) for the 1982 rate of electoral participation (there were no state figures available at this writing). Among the Anglo population, the voice ratio in 1982 was 1,000 : 1,096. That is for every 1,000 Anglos who had registered to vote in the 1982 elections, there was nearly an equal number not registered. Some were children, and a very few were not citizens, hence they could not have registered. Others did not register for a variety of reasons. The outcome was near-equivalence between those who were in a position to participate and those who were not and whose concerns had to be carried by those participating if they were to be considered at all.

Among the Latino population, the voice ratio was much lower—1,000 : 3,196. For every 1,000 Latinos registered to vote, there were over three times as many who were not (for a variety of rea sons, to be discussed shortly). There are a great many nonparticipants and a very few participants in this population, which means that as a whole, its voice is very low. If Latino concerns are voiced only by Latino voters, then each such voter will need to speak for three other people. In the Anglo community, one voter need speak for only one other person.

Anglo voice high, Latino voice low—that is the current case. Let us look at compositional factors that go into creating high voice for the one group and low voice for the other. Then we can make some projections into the future to see how the movement toward an age-ethnic stratified society might affect the two voices.

Voting Rates

In a democracy such as ours voting is the principal means by which an individual or a group makes its voice heard. In this respect Latinos have been effectively silent. In the national elections of November 1982, for example, only 25.3 percent of eligible Latinos (age 18 and over) voted. This compares with 49.9 percent among the Anglos, a rate that was closely matched by Blacks, at 43.0 percent (USBC 1983a: 8).

This low rate of political participation among Latinos was not unique to those elections, but consistent with a historic and debilitating pattern. In the elections of 1978 the rate of Anglo voting was 46.9 percent, while the Latino rate was a dismal 23.5 percent (USBC 1979b: 8). Even the excitement of the presidential race of 1980, when Latinos were the target of registration campaigns, brought only a 29.9 percent Latino vote, against 60.9 percent for the Anglo population (USBC 1981: 3).

In great part these figures represent not so much a low turnout on election day as an extremely low rate of voter registration. Nationally, Anglos of eligible age registered at almost twice the rate of Latinos in 1982 (65.5% vs. 35.3%; USBC 1983a: 8). This differential, moreover, is preserved at the regional level in areas of high Latino population. The Southwest Voter Registration Education Project, for example, found Anglos in the Southwest registering at a rate of 63.5 percent in 1976, and Latinos at only 34.9 percent (Hernandez 1977: 3). Many other studies over a period of years have confirmed this finding (Rose Institute 1980).

These voting patterns have been of little concern to society at large in the past (Riddell 1980; Santillan 1980). But in terms of the need for social cohesion in the near future, when difficult policy choices will have to be made, raising Latinos' rate of participation must become the focus of considerable effort. If Latinos do not feel they are well represented, they might see—and understandably chafe under—the support of the elderly as a burden imposed on them. Therefore, it is prudent to understand some of the inputs to the low levels of voter registration and participation among this increasingly important group.

Compositional Effects

The low Latino ratio is due in good part to the very composition of the Latino population. If one were to select 1,000 Latinos and 1,000 Anglos at random, and compare the two samples, one would find that the very demographic composition of the Latino population creates the conditions for a low voice. These compositional elements include a high proportion of immigrants, a low rate of naturalization, a high proportion of children, low income, low education, and low occupation. We do not intend to provide a causal model for low Latino voice, but we do wish to emphasize some of the major demographic elements at work in muting that voice.

Immigration. Only a generation or so ago the United States was a country of immigrants. But that is no longer true. In 1979 94.5 percent of the U.S. population was native-born and hence eligible by reason of birth to register and vote. At that time, by contrast, 30.3 percent of the nation's Latino population was foreign-born (USBC 1980: 10). This means that from the very start, nearly a third of the Latinos (and perhaps more) are ineligible to vote unless they choose to go through the lengthy process of naturalization.

California, if not exactly a state of immigrants, certainly has many more foreign-born than the national average. In 1980 15.1 percent of Californians were foreign-born, and the proportion has been increasing annually. In part this is because the rate of foreign-born among the Latino population is substantially higher than the national average—37.0 percent. Because of the high number of Latino (and Asian) newcomers, it might be more instructive to look at other segments of the state's population. The Anglo population was only 7.4 percent foreign-born, and the Black population only 2.5 percent (EDD 1986: 10). It is easy to see why both groups, composed primarily of natural-born citizens, should register and vote in the numbers they do.

Citizenship. In the context of political participation, the rate at which Latinos become naturalized citizens is an area for concern. In 1982 over 66 percent of the immigrants from Europe had taken out citizenship. This compares with only 21 percent of legally eligible foreign-born Latinos. And among those born in Mexico (about 80% of all foreign-born Latinos), only 18.2 percent had become naturalized citizens (USBC 1983b: Table 194).

Again, this pattern is not unique to California. In the five-year period from 1976 to 1981, people of Mexican origin accounted for 13.4 percent of all legal immigrants to the United States but for only 4.8 percent of all naturalizations (U.S. Immigration and Naturalization Service 1982: 4, 54). A national survey of people of Mexican origin in 1979 showed that only 5.0 percent of those born in Mexico had become citizens (Arce 1982). Even though California Latinos take out citizenship at a comparatively high rate, the rate is still far below that of the European-born. The failure to become citizens, then, obviously reduces the potential pool of Latino voters to a considerable extent.

Age and education. Study after study has shown that all across the country, young people are less likely to register and vote than their elders (Campbell et al. 1960; Scammon & Wattenberg 1971). As indicated in Figure 7.1, only 24.8 percent of the 18–24 age group voted in the 1982 national elections, compared with 62.2 percent of those aged 45–64 and fully 59.9 percent of those aged 65 and over.

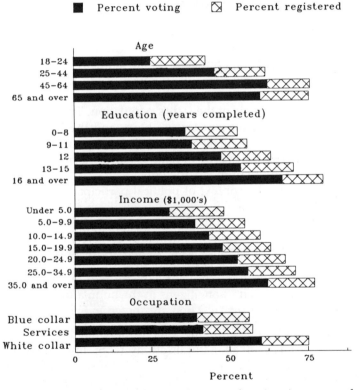

Fig. 7.1. Voting and registration rates by age, education, income, and occupation, United States, 1982. Source: U.S. Bureau of the Census, *Voting and Registration in the Election of November, 1982* (Washington, D.C., 1983).

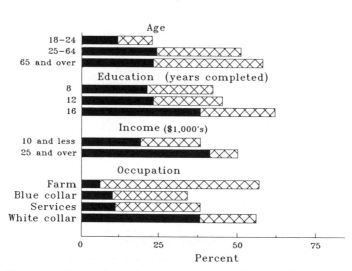

Fig. 7.2. Latino and non-Latino voting rates by age, education, income, and occupation, United States, 1978. Source: U.S. Bureau of the Census, *Voting and Registration in the Election of November, 1978* (Washington, D.C., 1979).

The age structure of the Latino population goes far to explain its low voice. With a median age of 23.1 years, we would expect the rates to be depressed simply because young people of whatever ethnicity are less likely to vote than older people. But also, as one would expect, Latino participation, even when controlled for age, is much lower than non-Latino, because of the high proportion of immigrants and noncitizens in the population.

The results of the 1978 election are shown in Figure 7.2. As we see, at every age level the national Latino population voted at about half the rate of the non-Latino population. In the 18–24 age group only 11.5 percent of Latinos voted, against 24.3 percent of the non-Latinos. And in the age-65-and-over bracket, 24.9 percent of Latinos voted (a very small number in absolute terms, to be sure), compared with 56.7 percent of the non-Latinos (USBC 1979a).

Another characteristic of the general electorate is the tendency for people to vote at increasingly higher rates as their level of education increases (Nie et al. 1976). This trend can be clearly seen in both Figure 7.1 and Figure 7.2. In the 1982 elections only 35.7 percent of those with eight years or less of education voted, compared with 66.5 percent of college graduates. The 1978 results indicate that Latinos, even when controlled for education, participated at well under half the rate of the general electorate: only 20.3 percent for those with eight years of education, and only 36.5 percent for college graduates.

Income and occupation. Again, in the U.S. electorate, we find a tendency for voting rates to climb as income increases. Returning to Figures 7.1 and 7.2, we see that only 38.7 percent of workers earning less than $10,000 voted in the 1982 election, against a full 62 percent of those earning $35,000 and over. Here again Latinos in the same income brackets voted at much lower rates. Barely 17.8 percent of those earning less than $10,000 voted in 1978, and only 41.9 percent of those earning $25,000 or more.

Turning, finally, to the voting patterns of the different occupational groups, we notice a familiar trend. People in lower-status occupations vote less often than those in higher-status ones. In Figure 7.1 we see that in the 1982 elections, only 39.1 percent of blue-collar workers voted, as compared with 57.8 percent of white-collar workers. And again Latinos of the same occupational level voted at considerably lower rates: 19.5 percent for blue-collar workers, and only 36.3 percent for white-collar workers. One interesting difference is to be found in the farming occupation, where fully 50.7 percent of non-Latinos voted, but only 9.6 percent of Latinos.

General trends. To summarize these statistics, a college graduate who is engaged in the professions, who earns over $25,000 a year, and who is 45 or older is the person most likely to register and vote. Conversely, the person least likely to vote is an unskilled laborer who has eight years or less of schooling, earns less than $7,500 a year, and is no more than 24 years old. (See Hill & Luttbeg 1983 for a full study of U.S. voting behavior.) It is clear that the average Latino is likely to resemble the less active voter on all counts: education, occupation, income, and age. But beyond that, he or she is also likely to be ineligible to vote for lack of citizenship.

These, when considered all together, are the compositional effects. By virtue of the very nature of the Latino population's socioeconomic and demographic characteristics, its voice is low.

Yet all is not bleak. There is one area in which Latinos do quite well. Though it is true that they are less likely to register than the rest of the population, there is significant evidence that those who do register vote at rates equal to, or greater than, the rest of the electorate. In the 1982 elections, for example, 71.1 percent of all the Latinos who were registered to vote did so, close to the Anglo figure of 76.1 percent. According to figures developed by Arce, 85.4 percent of registered Latinos could be expected to vote (Arce 1982). And data from other sources confirm that registered Latinos tend to vote at rates of at least 65 percent to 73 percent (Gonzalez Meza 1981). In short, however difficult it may be for Latinos to register, once they take that step, they are as likely as anyone else to vote.

In this connection groups such as the Southwest Voter Registration Education Project, the Mexican American Legal Defense and Education Fund (MALDEF), and Proyecto Participar have noted this high turnout and have concentrated particularly on increasing the Latinos' rate of registration. Thanks to such efforts, their registration increased 38 percent between the 1976 and 1980 elections, and their voter participation 23 percent (Gonzalez Meza 1981). These groups feel that a substantial increase in the number of registered Latinos alone will make the politicians sit up and take notice.

And yet there is a downside to this increase in participation. There are large numbers of undocumented in the Latino population of California. Chances are that many, perhaps most, of these people do not figure in the census data or in Latino-specific surveys, such as Arce's national Chicano survey. Many of these immigrants work and pay taxes of all sorts, tax monies that in the future may well be in large part diverted to the elderly in one form or another of income transfer. For the undocumented, there is no way in which their voice may be heard in the electoral process.

The lot of the undocumented indeed is taxation without representation. The tax burden will increase in the future, as the elderly's support needs grow, and under current policy this important population segment will have no voice. Unlike Hirschman's consumers, the undocumented will have no voice and no choice for exit. One can only be concerned about their loyalty, from the standpoint of social cohesion and willingness to be taxed heavily, when they have been denied basic services such as education for themselves and their children.

The effects of the demographic and socioeconomic composition of the Latino population may be seen in a tangible outcome: elected official representation. If there were no barriers, one could reasonably assume that Latino officials would be randomly distributed in various offices at about the same rate as Latinos are distributed in the general population, i.e., about 20 percent of all elected officials should be Latino. As we have become accustomed to finding, there is a shortfall between what one would expect and what one actually finds. In 1980 only 4.8 percent of the mayors in the state of California were Latino; of county supervisors, 5.4 percent; of state assemblypersons, 3.8 percent; and of state senators, 7.5 percent (Mexican American Legal Defense and Education Fund 1981). Since the setting of electoral boundaries may affect the Latino representation, these low percentages may not be due solely to low levels of registration and voting. Nonetheless, the shortfall is real. In absolute numbers there should have been 84 Latino mayors in 1980, not just 20; 59 county supervisors, not 16; 16 assemblypersons, not 3; and 8 state senators, not 3.

Nonelectoral Political Participation

Such low rates of political participation are, to a certain extent, the result of earlier social and political processes. After the U.S. annexation of Mexican territory, when California was preparing to apply for statehood, eight of the 48 delegates to the state constitutional convention were Mexican. The original constitution was written in both Spanish and English. One of the first governors of California was a Mexican (not surprising, considering the territory had always had Mexican governors while it was politically part of the Mexican Republic), as were many legislators. Officially, California was a bilingual state. Unofficially, however, legislative measures, prejudice, and outright fraud combined in the late nineteenth century to ensure little or no Latino political participation. These actions appear to have been successful.

But though essentially excluded from the formal political process since the state constitution was rewritten in 1879, Latinos have used other, nonelectoral means to attempt some measure of participation. Some attempts were of the "primitive rebel" type (Hobsbawm 1965), such as the resistance efforts of Tiburcio Vasquez and Joaquin Murrieta in the 1850's. Other, more formal attempts usually revolved around the founding of organizations to provide some voice, even if only to the Latino community itself. One of the first such organizations was formed in 1849, the Grupo Colonizador de Sonora.

During the late nineteenth and early twentieth centuries, most of these organizations were of a cultural bent. Beginning in the 1920's, however, more overtly political organizations were established. The League of United Latin American Citizens (LULAC), though founded in Texas, soon opened chapters in California. So did the American G.I. Forum, also founded in Texas (in 1946). The Mexican American Political Association (MAPA) was a California group from its inception in 1960.

The period of the 1960's and 1970's saw intense activity in the establishment of organizations to give voice to an otherwise unheard people. These were founded by community groups, by student groups, and eventually by professional groups. Some are focused on substantive issues such as health, education, or administration. Others are more generic, politically oriented community-organizing efforts.

Given the nature of the relations between the Latino population and the society at large, it is safe to say that any organization that labels itself as Latino has to engage, at some level, in political discourse. These organizations provide one type of forum where the concerns of the ineligible and the undocumented can be heard and discussed.

Projected Changes in Participation, 2030

Using our baseline assumptions, let us see how the Anglo and Latino voice ratios will change as the population changes. Superimposing 1982 national electoral participation rates over the age structure of the population in 2030, we find that by then 135 of every 1,000 Anglos will be ineligible to vote by reason of age and 16 by reason of noncitizenship, and that another 298 will not be registered, leaving only slightly over half, 551, registered and able to participate.

We project, then, that in 2030 the voice ratio for the Anglos will be 1,000 participants to 817 nonparticipants.

The political voice of the Latino population will continue to be comparatively low. Of every 1,000 Latinos in 2030, 249 will be under 18, 300 will not be citizens, and 174 will not be registered, although eligible, leaving 277 people who will register and perhaps participate. Thus, there will be fewer underage nonparticipants than in 1982 (458 per 1,000 Latinos), but more immigrant noncitizens (176 per 1,000). Overall the situation would improve, so that the Latino voice might be a bit louder: for every 1,000 Latino participants there will be 2,602 nonparticipants.

The participation rates presented earlier will no doubt change in the future. The Anglo elderly will almost certainly increase their participation. Whether the Latinos increase theirs is unpredictable; they might be compelled to do so by some sort of future social movement. Let us look first at what seems to us a certainty and then at the possibility.

The Elderly

When the Baby Boom generation retires, it will be the largest, best-educated, highest-income elderly generation in the nation's history. The demographic imperatives of age, education, and income will almost certainly increase the participation rate of this group. Moreover, it will have an added incentive to vote as more and more issues emerge centering on the specific concerns of old age as major political topics. Income maintenance, medical care, social care, nursing-home care, home health care—these and related matters will become the bread and butter issues for the elderly.

The Latinos

The recent increase in Latino political participation was, in large part, the result of the social movements of the 1960's. Few at the start of that decade could have foreseen the sudden upsurge of activity that by 1970 saw Latinos represented in education, health, and the legislative process. Much of this activity was stimulated by charismatic leaders who emerged in these years to organize movements aimed at working change in many different areas. The intensity of these movements had died down by the early 1980's.

It is possible that at some future date a similar resurgence of political passions, perhaps similarly sparked by a charismatic leader or activist organization, could lead to another quantum leap in participation. Such inspiration could persuade more immigrants to naturalize, more citizens to register, and more registered voters to go to the polls. Political funds, the lubrication of political machinery, could be raised in large amounts.

The directions such a social movement might take can only be speculated on. A movement might arise that would push for greater social cohesion, just as one might arise of a separatist bent. It seems safe to say that any movement that developed as a protective mechanism against discriminatory groups and measures aimed against Latinos and minorities could only contribute to social disintegration. On the other hand, one that developed in a positive context could contribute immeasurably to the political and social life of the state.

Policy Areas for Consideration

Our brief analysis of the effects of the Latino population's composition on its rates of political participation suggests a number of policy areas that need further work.

1. Naturalization. For a population that is at least 37 percent foreign-born and slow to naturalize, an effort to increase the naturalization rate is imperative. To this end, we badly need further research on the practice of allegiance switching, and the reasons why people do or do not become citizens.

2. Voter registration. The number of Latinos registering to vote appears to be increasing. As noted earlier, the Southwest Voter Registration Project and other groups have demonstrated that concentrated efforts can bear fruit. These efforts need to be better understood and more often replicated. There is always the possibility that some future charismatic leader can inspire more Lati-

nos to register (perhaps even to become naturalized), but that possibility is obviously no basis for long-range (or even short-term) policy.

3. The ineligible and the undocumented. It is a fact of political life that there are and will continue to be large numbers of ineligible and undocumented people in the population. Their concerns simply cannot be ignored. Some means of seeking out and considering their political views needs to be found. This may take the form of including nonelectoral political organizations when policy is formulated. Or it could take the form of appointive commissions, boards, and agencies whose purpose would be to express, in an advisory fashion, the concerns of those without a political voice.

4. Social cohesion and bloc voting. Demographic trends that will substantially change the composition of the electorate need to be recognized. Social cohesion will have to be at its highest, we believe, if the difficult policy questions of elderly support are to be answered pacifically. Society cannot afford to become polarized into "we" and "they" across generational and ethnic lines. The issues cannot be polarized, and political strategies of the future cannot be based on bloc voting. Latinos will be at a political disadvantage, yet they must make the wheels of commerce turn. The ability of the younger generation to support the older must be accompanied by the will to do so. And that will cannot be bludgeoned out of any group: it must develop naturally and be given freely. Equal representation is the cornerstone of a representative democracy. This implies that issues involving the elderly must be linked to issues affecting the lives of the Latinos and other minorities. A comprehensive policy has to be developed aimed at preserving social cohesion. No long-range political strategy can afford to depend on the political weakening of the Anglo or on the continuing political weakness of the Latino.

Chapter Eight

The National Outlook

To this point we have concentrated on the demographic future of the state of California and examined the policy issues that are bound to arise as it becomes an age-ethnic stratified society. We would like to turn our attention now to the question of such a development as a national phenomenon. One aspect of this is, of course, demographic change. Also pertinent at the national level are the related issues of immigration and assimilation. On the issue of immigration we would like to suggest a new way to consider the current and future influx of people from Latin America: as an interactive process in which the historical and continuing relationships between the sending countries and the United States play a crucial role. The other issue has to do with the kind of cultural transformation that may take place in the United States under the impact of a new ethnic mix. Profound changes of many sorts seem to us both inevitable and desirable under the appropriate circumstances.

National Latino Population Distribution, 1980

California is not the only state with a rapidly growing Latino population. The same kind of growth is taking place in Arizona, Colorado, New Mexico, Texas, Illinois, the New York and New Jersey area, and Florida, among others. But such states as Montana, Iowa, and Minnesota (to name just a few) have relatively few Latino residents and are not likely to attract many more in the future. So we may properly wonder what the national picture might look like in the next century when some states have large populations of young Latinos and others do not. We will begin with an overview of the current Latino population distribution. As may be seen in Figure 8.1, the U.S. Latino population is concentrated in particular areas of the country. There are small pockets of Latinos all across the country, but the 1980 census found that almost 72 percent of those counted (some 14.7 million all told) lived in just five states: California, Texas, New York, Florida, and Illinois.

A state-by-state breakdown of the 1980 data gives a clue to possible future trends. At that time California had 4.5 million Latinos (or 30.8% of the total), Texas 2.9 million (19.8%), New York 1.7 million (11.4%), Florida 0.8 million (5.8%), and Illinois 0.6 million (4.1%; Valdez & Viera 1983).

As we saw in an earlier chapter, this population is far from homogeneous. Like their countries of origin, the various Latino sub-

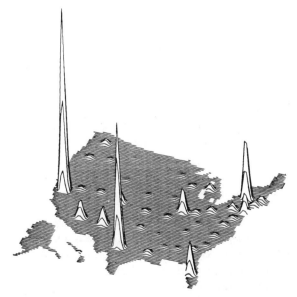

Fig. 8.1. Distribution of the Latino population, United States, 1980.
Source: U.S. Bureau of the Census, *Persons of Spanish Origin by State: 1980* (Washington, D.C., 1982), p. 6. Figs. 8.2–8.4 are from the same source.

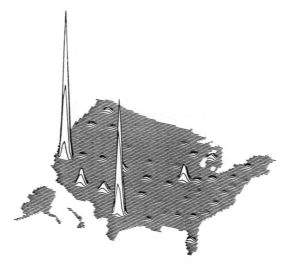

Fig. 8.2. Distribution of the Mexican-origin Latino population, United States, 1980

groups differ markedly in many respects. Though there are many subgroups, for our purposes we need only concern ourselves with the three main ones: those made up of people of Mexican, Puerto Rican, and Cuban origin. (In the following discussion we dispense with the cumbersome term "origin." "Mexicans," then, means all people of that origin, whether U.S.-born or not.)

Mexicans. Mexicans are by far the largest Latino subgroup in the United States, numbering 8.7 million in 1980, or 60 percent of all Latinos. Since it is widely agreed that undocumented people were severely undercounted in the census, this figure may be well off the mark. As we see in Figure 8.2, Mexicans are concentrated in the West and Southwest, especially Texas and California. Some 83 percent resided in California, Arizona, New Mexico, Texas, and Colorado in 1980. The only other state with a significant Mexican population is Illinois.

In 1980 the Mexican population had a median education of about 9.2 years, a median annual income of $13,439, and a median age of 22 years (Guernica & Kasperuk 1982: 60–62). This is the fastest growing of the Latino subgroups, showing an increase of 83 percent between the 1970 and 1980 censuses.

Puerto Ricans. Puerto Ricans form the second largest Latino sub-group in the United States, with a population of 2.0 million in 1980. They are concentrated in two main areas: New York–New Jersey (61% in 1980) and Illinois (20%; Valdez & Viera 1983). The rest of the group is distributed across the country, with small concentrations in California and Florida (see Fig. 8.3). The Puerto Ricans had a median education of about 9.0 years, an annual median income of $8,787, and a median age of 20 years in 1980. This population grew by 41 percent between 1970 and 1980.

Cubans. The Cuban subgroup is quite different from the two other main Latino subgroups. It is the smallest of the three, with a census count of 803,226 in 1980. Moreover, it is heavily concentrated in just one state—Florida. Some 59 percent of the Cubans in the United States live there; most of the others live in the New York–New Jersey area and California (see Fig. 8.4). This subgroup differs significantly from the others in age (median, 37 years in 1980), education (12.2 years), and income ($15,342; Guernica & Kasperuk 1982). Between 1970 and 1980 this population grew by 48 percent.

These three subgroups together accounted for roughly 11.6 million of the 14.7 million Latinos who were covered in the 1980 census.

Fig. 8.3. Distribution of the Puerto Rican–origin Latino population, United States, 1980

Fig. 8.4. Distribution of the Cuban-origin Latino population, United States, 1980

A national-origin breakdown is not useful for the 3.1 million other Latinos, since no single Latin American country is significantly represented among them. These people are distributed across the country pretty much in the manner of the overall Latino population, that is, with large numbers living in California and the Southwest and small concentrations in Illinois, the New York and New Jersey area, and Florida.

Latino Growth Nationally

We do not have the data or resources that would be required to replicate our California analysis for the other 49 states, and each state has unique characteristics that any credible analysis must take into account. However, we can present an informed speculation on the general shape of the U.S. population based on two demographic trends that are certain to influence the national population picture for at least the next 50 years.

First, the Latino population will continue to grow through fertility and immigration. Fertility may well decrease, but probably not to current Anglo levels. The reconstitution of families of undocumented immigrants given amnesty, temporary worker programs, U.S. military involvement in Central America, and the economic instability of Mexico are all reasons why immigration will continue to be a factor in Latino population growth. Second, because of lower fertility and the age concentration in the Baby Boom generation, the Anglo population will continue to age; that is, there will be high concentrations of Anglos in the older ages and low concentrations in the younger age groups.

The U.S. Bureau of the Census first published projections of the national Latino population in late 1986. Following its usual procedure, the bureau based its projections on low, middle, and high fertility, mortality, and immigration assumptions. We are heartened by the fact that these middle-range assumptions are substantially similar to our California baseline assumptions and by the fact that the bureau's findings for the nation are also similar. In respect to the relative size of Latinos and Anglos, the highlights of the national projections are as follows:

1. The Latino population may double within 30 years and triple in 60.

2. Even without international migration, the Latino population may grow more quickly than would most other major population groups with immigration.

3. The Anglo population may peak in size by 2020 and then steadily decrease.

4. The Anglo proportion of the total population may decline in the future.

In short the Census Bureau (1986: 1) predicts a demographic future for Latinos nationwide similar to the one we have previously presented in detail for California.

The economic future is less predictable, and it can be strongly influenced by variations in state and local economies. But several considerations seem fairly certain. Latinos' lower educational attainment will have an adverse impact on economic productivity. This will happen at the same time that Latinos are becoming a larger part of the working-age population. These factors will shape the economic well-being of the states where Latinos are concentrated. As Latinos become a larger part of the total national population and work force, national income and revenue figures could be adversely affected.

Latinos are currently concentrated in a few states, and this uneven distribution is likely to continue into the future. The age-ethnic gap that we project in California is likely to occur in other states with current concentrations of Latinos, and the aggregate projected change can lead to important regional and national differences.

States with Latino Growth

Any state that had at least a 15 percent Latino representation in its population in 1980 and will have at least a 30 percent representation in 2030 is likely to be age-ethnically stratified if that Latino population is either Mexican or Puerto Rican, or both. In addition to California, there are four states that fit these criteria: New Mexico, Texas, Arizona, and Colorado. Let us see what the future might hold for each.

New Mexico. In 1980 45 percent of the population was Latino. In fact, Latinos were the majority population until after the Second World War. Most of these people are from families that emigrated from the south (Mexico) in the sixteenth and seventeenth centuries. There has been some, but not much, immigration from Mexico since the late nineteenth century, with what appears to have been an upswing from the 1960's onward. A state with a total population of 1.3 million would not require a large amount of immigration for Latinos to become the majority population again. It is likely that this state has been marked by age-ethnic stratification since 1985.

Texas. In 1980 21.4 percent of the state's population was Latino (2.9 million in a total of 13.5 million), largely of Mexican origin. In macro-economic terms Texas is very similar to California, and we would expect that in all respects—age-ethnic stratification, employment, income, education, health, and political participation—the outcome there in 2030 will be very close to what we have projected for California.

Arizona. In 1980 20.9 percent of Arizona's population was Latino, largely of Mexican origin (in absolute terms, 0.5 million Latinos in a total population of 2.5 million). There is significant immigration from Mexico. There is also a significant "snowbird migration," a skewed in-migration of Anglo elderly seeking retirement in the sun. It is probable that the age-ethnic stratification will be intensified here.

Colorado. This state is just under the cutoff, with a 13.7 percent Latino representation in 1980. Its total population is relatively

small, at 2.7 million. A very small increase in the Latino population would easily make this state subject to the same considerations as the other states above.

There are three other states that do not meet both of our criteria, but have the potential to tend in the same direction—New
York, Illinois, and Florida.

New York. In 1980 the state had a total of 17.8 million people, of
whom 1.7 million (8.9%) were Latinos. Because these are largely
Puerto Ricans, the Latino population is a young one. However,
since Puerto Rico, the major sending area, has only a small population base (3.8 million in 1980), immigration from Puerto Rico
cannot approach the magnitude of immigration from Mexico. The
other Latinos in the state are mostly from South American subgroups that tend to be of higher class origin, better educated,
older, and less fertile. These characteristics mitigate the chances
of rapid Latino population growth. Thus New York will probably
fall short of feeling the full effects of an age-ethnic stratification.

Illinois. There is a significant Latino population in Illinois (0.6
million, or 5.4% of the 11.0 million total population in 1980).
About 60 percent of this Latino population is of Mexican origin
and about 25 percent Puerto Rican. It is young, with high fertility.
The state appears to get direct immigration from Mexico. Although Illinois will not show the same degree of age-ethnic stratification as the states with higher concentrations of Mexican-origin
Latinos, it will have something of that flavor.

Florida. Of this state's 9.3 million inhabitants, 0.8 million, or
8.6 percent, are Latino. However, because most of these people
are Cubans or South Americans, with a much higher median age,
income, and education and a lower fertility than the Mexicans
and Puerto Ricans, growth of the Latino population will not result
in age-ethnic stratification in Florida, barring significant immigration from Mexico or Puerto Rico.

States with Aging Anglo Growth

Just as we did with the states with high Latino concentrations,
we set two criteria for identifying states where there are signs of
an aging Anglo population with virtually no young Latinos: (1) at
least 15 percent of the population must have been age 60 and over
in 1980, with the prospect of having 25 to 30 percent elderly (per-

haps as high as 35 percent in some areas) by 2010 to 2030; and (2) the Latino population was 5 percent or less of the total in 1980.

Social Security projections, covered in Chapter 2, show that by 2020 approximately 22 percent of the nation's population will be 65 and over. But certain states will have a larger share of elderly (60 years or older) in their populations than others. In 1980, for example, some states already had between 15 percent and 20 percent of their population age 60 and older: Minnesota (18.6%), South Dakota (18.1%), Nebraska and Iowa (18.0%), Kansas (17.6%), and North Dakota (15.9%).

What are the implications for the country as the demographic disparity between regions grows sharper? It seems clear that the intergenerational income transfer could also become an inter-regional transfer.

If current projections are correct, and the sun belt states are where much of the nation's future growth will take place, this intergenerational, interregional income transfer could grow to imposing proportions. Those states clearly correlate with the high Latino concentration states, so that any national program for the support of the elderly based on the taxation of income would see great amounts of money siphoned off from that region.

Immigration

One of the most notable differences between earlier patterns of U.S. immigration and the pattern today is the westward tilt in the receiving areas. Los Angeles and San Francisco today play the role in receiving immigrants that New York and other eastern cities played in the late nineteenth and early twentieth centuries. In part this has to do with another important difference: the current immigration draws very little from the customary European countries; the largest numbers of immigrants today are Latin Americans and Asians, both of whom tend to settle in the West and the Southwest.

The principal sources of immigration to California are typical of this trend. In 1980 fewer than a fifth of the 3,580,033 immigrants counted in the census were from Europe. As can be seen in Figure 8.5, the largest single sending region by far was Latin America, which supplied close to half of all immigrants. The next-

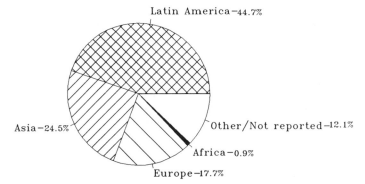

Fig. 8.5. Area of origin of immigrants in California, 1980. Source: U.S. Bureau of the Census, *Detailed Population Characteristics: California* (Washington, D.C., 1983), Table 195, pp. 6–9.

largest, Asia, sent about a quarter, and the rest of the world (including Canada) accounted for something under 13 percent (a figure that includes those not reporting their nationality).

In essence the new immigration may be characterized as a Pacific Rim immigration: 73.7 percent of California's immigrants came from one or other Rim country (including Canada; USBC 1983b: 6–9).

Latin American Sending Countries

In 1980, 1,600,716 foreign-born Latinos resided in California. Of these, the vast majority (1,277,966, or 79.8%) were from Mexico. The four next largest suppliers were El Salvador, Cuba, Guatemala, and Argentina, which together accounted for fewer than 200,000 people (see Table 8.1).

Since 1980 political instability has led to an increase in immigration of felt but unmeasured proportions from Guatemala, El Salvador, Honduras, and Costa Rica. Meanwhile, immigration from Mexico has continued apace. About half of all Mexican migrants head for California; and the larger share of the others settle in Texas or Illinois (Zazueta 1980).

The number of Latin American immigrants in the state (and the country) is of course higher than these figures indicate. The size of the undocumented population is simply unknown.

TABLE 8.1
Latin American Immigrants to California by Country of Origin, 1980

Country	Number	Country	Number
Mexico	1,277,966	Ecuador	13,130
El Salvador	67,656	Brazil	7,357
Cuba	46,258	Guyana	2,102
Guatemala	35,046	Other Central	
Argentina	20,789	American	60,348
West Indies	16,673	Other South	
Colombia	16,256	American	22,067
Peru	15,068		

SOURCE: U.S. Bureau of the Census, *Detailed Population Characteristics: California* (Washington, D.C., 1983), pp. 6–9.

TABLE 8.2
Asian Immigrants to California by Country of Origin, 1980

Country	Number	Country	Number
Philippines	237,713	India	30,010
China	116,331	Israel	15,744
Vietnam	83,272	Thailand	15,462
Korea	83,180	Lebanon	14,192
Japan	79,593	Turkey	11,793
Iran	49,083	Other Asian	107,200
Hong Kong	33,300		

SOURCE: Same as Table 8.1.

Asian Sending Countries

There were 876,878 foreign-born Asians in the state in 1980. As we saw earlier, the state's Asian population has a significantly higher median education and income than the other minority groups. Indeed, the Asian population occupies a unique niche in California's professional and business life. Because Asians are quite likely to play a critical role in the state's future, much greater than mere numbers would indicate, in a chapter dealing with immigration and culture we must give more heed to this group than we have to this point.

In 1980 the Philippines was the most important Asian sending country (237,713 immigrants), followed by China, Vietnam, Korea, and Japan (see Table 8.2). Since 1980 the state's Southeast

Asian population has grown substantially, the result of the "secondary immigration" of Vietnamese, Laotians, and Cambodians who settled in other parts of the country on first coming to the United States. Perhaps as many as two-thirds of all the nation's Southeast Asians may now live in California, primarily in Orange County (near Los Angeles) and San Jose. There is also a sizable Asian population of undocumented immigrants.

Thanks to the movies and television, in the popular imagination California's population consists of blond, tanned Midwesterners-turned-surfers. The data, however, show that it is becoming a population of foreign-born immigrants, as New York's was in the early years of this century, but drawn now from Latin America and Asia, not Europe.

The Trajectory of Immigration

Because the population projections presented earlier are sensitive to immigration, the likely future of immigration merits some attention.

Immigration is not merely a random movement of individuals from one place to another. Were that the case, immigration would form a sort of random or "Brownian motion" in which there would be no discernible net gains or losses. Further, immigration is more than the aggregation of individual decisions and situations. It needs to be understood as the result of structural relations between the sending and receiving areas.

The classic model of immigration posits push factors in the sending country and pull factors in the receiving one. The push factors create a population that is likely to emigrate, and the pull factors attract that population to a particular area.

We would like to suggest that another level of complexity needs to be added to the push-pull model of immigration in order to better understand the present and future situation. This complexity is that the push and pull factors do not always operate simultaneously and independently, but in some cases are very much related to one another. That is, in some cases the push factors in the sending country may be linked to the pull factors in the receiving one.

In the case of Latin American immigration, there has been a unique linkage between the push factors in Mexico and Latin America and the pull factors in the United States. This unique linkage has not been shared to the same degree by any other sending region in the world. This linkage has its roots in the Monroe Doctrine, first pronounced in 1823, in which the United States declared all of Latin America to be within its sphere of interest. The Latino population was originally acquired by armed conquest, which from the beginning provided a different attitude to immigration from Mexico and Latin America than the non-militarily influenced immigration from Europe (Hayes-Bautista & Chapa 1987).

The structural relations between the United States and Europe were diverse: the more industrialized countries sent both capital and population to the United States, and the less industrialized ones merely sent population without the complication of any further economic or military ties. In general the relations between the United States and the European nations were close to relations between equals, with perhaps Europe having a greater influence on the United States (via its capital and immigrant population) than the United States had on Europe. However, in the relations between the United States and Mexico and other Latin American countries, the relations were different: the United States has had a much greater effect on those nations in a nearly completely unilateral sense than they have had on the United States.

No one would deny that the United States has had, and continues to have, a profound influence on the economic and political structures of its Latin American neighbors, especially Mexico and the other countries of Central America. Since we are concerned with the future in this volume, we will avoid the long history of direct U.S. political involvement in the region except to note the prominent role that military occupation or the threat of it has played in that history, from the U.S.-Mexican War to the Bay of Pigs (for detailed history, see Herring 1968).

The history of indirect political involvement is just as long, and the 1980's have not seen the end of it. It manifests itself in its most

extreme form in the support of the Contras in their effort to over-
throw the government of Nicaragua. Less familiar and less obvious is the pressure the United States can—and does—apply to
get Latin American states to create economic blockades of countries out of favor such as Cuba.

Finally, direct and indirect economic relationships heavily influence all aspects of economic and policy life in Latin America.
The most spectacular case would be the foreign debt problems of
Mexico and other Latin American countries, which have necessarily rippled down through their business communities—touch-
ing every firm with an outstanding loan, for example.

In sum, unlike the push and pull factors involved in the European immigration, those between the United States and Latin
America are intricately intertwined and much more unilateral. By
heavily influencing the course of economic development and the
political processes in Latin America, the United States has created
or exacerbated the push conditions in the sending countries: the
antiquated economic structures that cannot provide employment
to the population; the governments that force their citizens to flee
for their lives; and the dramatic population growth that has led
to a near quadrupling of the people of Central America since
the 1930's.

As of this writing (1987) a major piece of immigration legislation has been approved, the Simpson-Rodino bill. Though regula-
tions have yet to be written, and the constitutionality of various
portions of the law tested in courts, a number of early commen-
tators on the proposed law felt that in the long run the volume of
immigration would not be greatly affected (McCarthy 1986; Kimball et al. 1986). It is our opinion that demand for imported labor
will increase in the future (McCarthy & Valdez 1985), and that the
economic crisis in Mexico will continue to be nearly insurmount-
able (Rivas 1985) because of the foreign debt issue, creating conditions that will feed immigration for the foreseeable future. Legislation such as the Simpson-Rodino bill will serve to make the
individual's situation more difficult, but does not, in our opinion,
even begin to address the international aspects of immigration. In

our judgment immigration is not strictly a domestic issue, but also a foreign policy one. Given the reluctance with which the United States has dealt directly with Mexico and Latin America, it appears that domestically focused legislation, which will not achieve the intended effect, will continue to be the focused effort. This means that immigration will continue, and the baseline projections will most likely not be affected.

Assimilation, Culture, and Identity

The idea of immigrant assimilation is a dominant recurring theme in popular American thought. The meaning, goal, or content of assimilation has changed over the course of American history. There are three prevalent interpretations of assimilation that have been important in American history: Anglo-conformity, the melting pot, and cultural pluralism.

The meaning of *Anglo-conformity* is implied in the term itself: the immigrant group is expected to take on language and cultural patterns based on English traditions. This point of view was often associated with prejudice against all immigrants who were not Protestants from Northern or Western Europe. Racism was often, but not universally, a component of the beliefs of Anglo-conformists. However, the belief in the superiority of Anglo-Saxon culture and institutions was the defining aspect of this theory of assimilation. The prominence of Anglo-conformity was historically linked with periods of anti-immigrant nativism (Gordon 1964: 88–114).

The idea of the *melting pot* was more liberal, open, and optimistic than Anglo-conformity. The result of America's immigration was seen as a new culture and, often, a new people—Americans rather than English, Italian, or whatever. The new people would result from intermarriage and amalgamation, the new culture from the fusion of the old and new (Gordon 1964: 115–31).

Cultural pluralism holds that it is preferable for an immigrant group to maintain its language, culture, and endogamy while still participating in the larger society. Assimilation, as it is generally used, connotes either Anglo-conformity or the melting pot. Cultural pluralism is a reaction to these and can be said to be an anti-assimilation ideology as much as a theory of assimilation (Novak 1972). Unlike Anglo-conformity and the melting pot, which have been popular ideas throughout this country's history, cultural pluralism was first put forward only in the twentieth century. Its original proponents were Jewish immigrants reacting against the ideals implicit in both of the other views of assimilation. They also argued that cultural pluralism described the history of immigrants better than the other views of assimilation (Gordon 1964: 132–59).

The idea of cultural pluralism became resurgent during the political upheaval of the 1960's. Racial and national minorities, including Mexicans and Puerto Ricans, proclaimed their rights to maintain and develop their own culture. And the European ethnics, who had supposedly been melted in the pot, soon followed them in clamoring for their right to maintain their own heritage.

All of these perspectives on assimilation tend to reify culture, to perceive it as something that has an existence of its own beyond the people who share it. We prefer to see culture as a social creation. It is the very embodiment of social relations and interactions (Berger & Luckmann 1967: 47; Schutz 1973: 10–14). Ethnicity and ethnic identity, too, are aspects of created culture (Portes & Bach 1985: 285–86).

These considerations go to the heart of our analysis. Few people conversant with demographic concepts will question the basic trends that we envision. While Latinos may not compose exactly 35.51 percent of California's population in 2030 and seniors may not compose exactly 22.35 percent as our baseline projection indicates, we expect general, if not unanimous, agreement on the magnitudes of these trends. The real question is, What will it mean to be Latino in the year 2030? Will Latinos be just part of the general population, or will they be distinct and different? Assimilationists would like to believe that the former will occur. It may, but Latinos currently are not assimilating economically. The degree of future identity with or apart from the rest of California's population is malleable; it can be changed by human actions, but the forging of this sense of loyalty is not what is in the cards now.

We began our book with a worst-case scenario, our conception of the current trends and tendencies. We will end it with a presentation of the policy window and the best-case scenario that may result from the implementation of appropriate policies. Once again we emphasize that demographic trends are not destiny. Rather, the future is very much what we make of it.

Chapter Nine

California in 2030: The Best-Case Scenario

In the preceding chapters we pointed to a number of policy areas to be dealt with. Urgency is imperative. In our estimation, there is a narrow policy window of about 15 to 20 years available on all of them: to wait until the year 2010 to become concerned about the health, education, and income-earning capacity of Latinos and other minorities will not do. Significant lead time is needed to achieve changes in the level of preparation of human resources. The social needs of the elderly will require attention as they arise in the near to midrange future: they cannot be postponed. But neither can the needs of the Latinos in our midst today, for as we hope we have demonstrated, the future of the one group is indisputably bound to the future of the other.

In the daily political framework, 15 years is a long time—a legislator can stand for reelection seven times. The electorate and politicians are often accused of looking no farther than the next election. The fulfillment of the intergenerational compact in the future will require the forging of an interethnic compact in the present. This will require that Latino and non-Latino politicians be identified, prepared, and involved in a 30-year policy process.

To provide an idea of the best that might happen as a result of such an effort, we offer now a best-case scenario. Like the worst-case scenario, it is extreme. But we remain optimistic.

The Scenario

By 1995 the growth of the Latino population in California was viewed with growing concern by the Anglo population. Spreading out from such areas of concentration as East Los Angeles, East San Jose, South San Diego, central Orange County, and the Mission District of San Francisco, Latino communities began to overflow into and then absorb many previously Anglo areas. Residential suburbs "turned" almost overnight, as Anglo homeowners left in a near-panic, hoping to sell their houses before a general property devaluation set in. New suburbs were pushed farther away from the city cores, requiring both the conversion of agricultural land and virgin desert to residential use and the development of increasingly elaborate systems to provide transportation and water to these areas far removed from the decaying cores.

The vast majority of these "urban refugees" were Baby Boomers. Life had been good to this generation. Hitting a vigorous mid-life stride, the Boomers were riding the crest of a wave of economic well-being. Their education was paying off, their income was high, and because they had few children, their discretionary spending was at an all-time high.

But just beneath the surface of a seemingly wealthy and thriving California were serious structural problems that threatened its stability. While the Latino population was growing, its participation in the state's economic, political, and cultural life was not welcomed. The passage of English-only laws was nearly a decade behind, but Spanish was still to be heard on the streets. The continuing linkages between the Latino population and Mexico and other Latin American countries was seen as a potential threat to societal cohesion. Latino emphasis on family life was seen as a quaint but functionless relic that impeded economic mobility.

Much of the growth in the Latino population was due to an unraveling situation in Mexico. The high foreign debt forced Mexico to spend upwards of $25 billion per year in debt service alone. This massive expenditure drained the country, making investment in business and human resources nearly impossible. While each year over a million persons entered the job market, virtually no new jobs were being created. The quality of life had been steadily deteriorating since the 1980's. Inflation raged at over 300 percent a year and the economy was unable to provide even the basic necessities of life for over half the country's population. Political stability was very much in question. U.S. television programs and movies pointed out to Mexicans, on a daily basis, the widening gap in living standards between the two countries.

Things were not completely well within the state of California either. The job market had become segmented, so that there were few positions in the higher paying, professional levels: the growth was in the poorly paid services sector. Anglos predominated in the upper segment, Latinos in the lower. Manufacturing in the state was in a weak position. Because of sporadic enforcement of the Simpson-Rodino immigration act of 1986, manufacturers were sometimes able to operate with a full labor force, but periodic sweeps and subsequent employer fines had made production difficult to budget and schedule. California's competitive position in the Pacific Rim economy was softening. Agricultural and raw forest and mineral products accounted for an increasingly large proportion of the total value of export goods, while sophisticated consumer goods continued to flood in from other Rim countries. Labor economists pointed out that the decline in educational expenditures in the 1970's and 1980's was now being reflected in a noticeable decline in the education level of the labor force. In short, the California economy seemed to be positioned for a long, slow, downwards slide. This condition led to an awakening and a transformation in society.

Thanks to the Affirmative Action programs of the 1970's and 1980's, there was a group of educators, physicians, dentists, attorneys, administrators, artists, scientists, clinical workers, researchers, planners, and businesspeople to give the state something that had been nearly totally lacking during the heyday of the Chicano movement in the 1960's—a critical mass of well-educated Latinos with a good understanding of their relation to their communities and their state. Drawing upon the experience of the veterans and the bases of community organization laid down in the 1960's and 1970's, these new Latino leaders were able to tap into a wellspring of symbolism and emotion that lurked just beneath the surface of many Latino communities. These leaders inspired Latino parents and youth to reach into themselves to strive for excellence and the highest levels of performance. Meanwhile, the Anglo Baby Boomers found their political voice in leaders who were able to rekindle the generational enthusiasm that, 30 years earlier, had led to a decade of selfless public service in such organizations as the Peace Corps and VISTA.

These two currents of interest—of the young Latinos and the aging Baby Boomers—converged in the development of a policy framework aimed at preserving the intergenerational compact through the development of an interethnic compact. The changing demographics of the state, leading to an age-ethnic stratified society, was becoming apparent to this group of leaders. But rather than see the growth of the Latino population as a problem, they came to see it as a solution to the problem of support for the aging Baby Boomers. Although some called it merely enlightened self-interest, both sets of leaders realized that an investment in the younger Latino population was the best guarantee of support for the elderly in the near future. Some even dared to call this policy a human rights policy—all members of society should have a chance to maximize their participation, irrespective of age or ethnicity.

The first major investment that had to be made was in the education of the younger, largely Latino population. Boosting educational achievement became a priority policy for the state. Probably the most important event in this effort was the emergence of a Latino intellectual tradition. The critical mass of Latino professionals provided a seedbed for the generation of excitement about exploring the intellectual tradition of Mexico and Latin America. Not only did the artists and humanists draw upon the old Latin American tradition, they helped to create the new Latino tradition. This new tradition served as a magnet, drawing out Latino youth and providing them with new horizons.

This new spirit was built upon by the policy makers. A new policy in bilingual education was adopted, mandating that graduating high school seniors be fluent in a major Pacific Basin foreign language. The public schools were open to all, regardless of legal status. The political commitment to quality education attracted Anglo students back into the public schools. Latino participation in higher education was not limited to the arts and humanities, and enrollment in math and science classes began to rise. The new attention to education helped to bring about the renewal of adult education, designed to raise the achievement level of former dropouts and immigrant parents, so that they could function better in the economy.

Side by side with this effort came an equally great investment in health. The coalition of Latino and Anglo leaders realized that the rapidly aging Baby Boomers would soon, by their sheer numbers, draw policy attention to their massive health care needs. The health needs of the younger, generally Latino population had to be served as well. A state-underwritten health insurance and services program called Soci-Cal was developed, providing for balanced services over a person's lifetime. In this way, the Latino needs for maternal and child health would balance the Anglo need for geriatrics. A major component of the plan was extensive health education and preventive health care.

The policy of investing in the state's future was not lost on business leaders. Confidence in the economy's future rose following the increase in expenditures for research at the university level. Basic business investment began to be made, halting a downward trend. The resulting increase in business activity brought about an expansion in the economy, which in turn necessitated a larger, better prepared work force. At the national level, spot shortages of labor around the country helped to create a climate in which a new immigration law was to be written. The prospect of a common market embracing Mexico, the United States, and Central America formed the basis for this new effort. This increased investment in Mexico and Central America created more jobs and boosted employment in that region. More people were enjoying greater income, and gradually the standard of living began to rise. Fertility dropped, and life expectancy increased. Emigration to the United States slowed.

California's improved business outlook was noted in many areas. Research and development spending improved, requiring ever more highly trained scientists and administrators. Increasingly, many of these were Latinos. Through quality education and comprehensive adult training programs, the wage gap between Anglos and Latinos closed.

Continuing a trend, Latino educational achievement continued to rise, until by 2030 it equaled Anglo achievement. The universities blossomed with new intellectual vigor, and California remained the academic center of the Pacific Basin region. Arts and sciences flourished, and did so bilingually. Latinos became fully represented in the sciences. Most important of all, a new intellectual tradition was becoming formalized.

The state health insurance program was expanded to cover income support, housing, social services, and death benefits for retiring California workers. The cost of this program was large, but the rising California economy was able to carry the expense. The younger, now highly productive, Latinos willingly shouldered the burden of support, for they felt that all inhabitants of the state were linked together regardless of age, gender, or ethnicity.

Their support was the result of a continuing societal commitment to Latino health and education. Public spending for education was seen as the key to generating sufficient economic growth to carry the Soci-Cal program in the future. The trajectory for rising Latino educational achievement had been discovered and merely required continuing attention.

After the year 2030, California society faced the future confidently. It was universally recognized all over the world as the model for twenty-first century society. Its economy and culture reflected a happy fusion of elements from Western Europe, Latin America, Asia, and Africa, leading to a new language, new social values, and even new forms of political dialogue. As that new decade began, California was the lead state for the other 49, and the lead society for other Pacific Rim societies. The future looked bright indeed.

Appendix

Appendix

Projections and Simulation Design

To provide alternative ways of estimating the burden of support during the end of the twentieth century and the beginning of the twenty-first, we developed three models. The first and most basic is a cohort-component demographic model, which has been used to project population by age, sex, and ethnic group. The components of change are live births, deaths, and net immigration. Alternative population projections are derived from differing assumptions for fertility rates, mortality rates, and net immigration levels. As measured by ratios of the senior population (65 and over) to the working-age population (16–64), for example, the population models provide one means of estimating the changing burden of support.

The second model developed is based on the first and projects the size of the labor force. Labor-force projections were similarly conducted for all age, sex, and ethnic-group cohorts and were derived from applying projected cohort-specific labor-force participation rates to corresponding cohort populations. This second model provides an alternative means of defining the burden of support based on the ratio of workers to nonworkers.

Since various groups of workers differ in their capacity to generate income and various types of nonwork income are received by different groups, a third model projects dollar income as expressed in constant 1985 dollars. This model provides a third measure of the burden of support, expressed in ratios of nonwork income to work income. The benefits of increased productivity can be evaluated with differing assumptions of real income growth rates.

The population projection model is the basis for the results presented in Chapters 2 and 3. The labor force and income projections are presented in Chapter 4. This Appendix discusses the data and methods used in the respective models. Comparisons are made with the population projections of other researchers.

Population Projections Model

In projecting population growth in California the three components of change are (1) fertility as expressed in live births to women of childbearing age, (2) mortality as reflected in cohort survival rates, and (3) estimated net migration, the difference between people moving into the state and those leaving. All projections developed for this work are based on the state's estimated baseline population for 1985. Individual cohorts are defined by sex (male and female), by age (five-year intervals from 0–4 years through 85–89 years, with a residual 90 years and older group), and by ethnicity (Anglos, Blacks, Asians, and Latinos, the last split into native-born and foreign-born groups). The rationale for disaggregating the population into this many groups is that fertility, mortality, and migration differ for the various cohorts; furthermore, as considered in subsequent models, labor-force participation and income levels differ for various groups.

Data used to calibrate the various models come from a variety of sources: cross-sectional data, such as from the 1980 Census Public Use Microdata Sample (PUMS), which provide highly detailed information on California age-specific and ethnic-specific fertility rates and the like; and published time-series data, such as from the U.S. Census Bureau's series of Current Population Survey (CPS) reports, which provide information on how the model parameters change over time, though often with less detail and with problems inherent in changing definitions and coverage.

The formula for the general cohort-change population model is Population (t_1) = Population (t_o) + Births (t) − Deaths (t) + Net Immigration (T), where t is the specific time period (five years in our model) between t_o (the starting point) and t_1 (the end point of the projection period). Calculations were made for each age-sex-ethnic cohort for each time-interval increment, and were successively generated, starting with the 1985 baseline data, for the years 1990, 1995, 2000, and so forth through 2030. Various outcomes were postulated by altering the assumptions regarding future fertility, mortality, and immigration.

Fertility

The data in Table A.1 reflect the fertility of California women by ethnicity from 1940 through 1980. More directly related to population projections are current fertility rates. Table A.2 shows total age-specific fertility rates derived from 1980 census data. These estimates, specifically prepared for this model, were determined by examining the mother-children relationships for a 5 percent sample of all females in California. Preliminary age- and ethnic-specific fertility rates were first derived and then proportionately adjusted by ethnic group, such that the resultant rates were consistent with the number of children listed as less than one

TABLE A.1
Total and Age-Specific Fertility Rates by Ethnicity, California, 1940–1980

Age and ethnic group	Married women 1940	Married women 1950	Married women 1960	Married women 1970	Married women 1980	All women 1970	All women 1980
Total all groups	*1.19*	*2.09*	*2.12*	*2.30*	*2.00*	*1.71*	*1.39*
15–19	0.40	0.95	0.75	0.61	0.62	0.11	0.09
20–29	0.76	1.65	1.83	1.48	1.16	1.14	0.78
30–39	1.24	2.25	2.47	2.81	2.07	2.65	1.90
40–49	1.60	2.49	2.12	2.79	3.01	2.68	2.89
Anglo total	*1.14*	*2.01*	*2.03*	*2.17*	*1.82*	*1.62*	*1.26*
15–19	0.38	0.90	0.70	0.55	0.52	0.09	0.06
20–29	0.73	1.59	1.74	1.38	0.97	1.06	0.62
30–39	1.18	2.20	2.37	2.67	1.87	2.52	1.71
40–49	1.55	2.31	2.03	2.64	2.73	2.53	2.62
Black total	*0.88*	*1.92*	*2.23*	*2.71*	*2.41*	*2.04*	*1.59*
15–19	0.50	1.68	1.16	0.86	0.67	0.23	0.14
20–29	0.88	1.92	2.22	2.02	1.46	1.65	1.01
30–39	0.70	2.13	2.61	3.24	2.36	3.10	2.16
40–49	1.07	1.60	1.87	3.21	3.49	3.11	3.41
Asian total	*2.47*	*2.24*	*2.23*	*2.22*	*1.97*	*1.55*	*1.36*
15–19	N.A.	0.58	1.00	0.45	0.65	0.06	0.08
20–29	1.05	1.42	1.51	1.29	1.13	0.76	0.72
30–39	1.94	2.56	2.47	2.34	1.96	2.17	1.76
40–49	4.40	3.82	2.84	2.81	3.03	2.63	2.90
Latino total	*2.25*	*3.25*	*2.89*	*3.02*	*2.61*	*2.16*	*1.86*
15–19	0.71	0.86	0.93	0.75	0.78	0.15	0.18
20–29	1.28	2.19	2.33	1.97	1.65	1.53	1.25
30–39	3.26	3.03	3.31	3.71	2.97	3.47	2.77
40–49	2.61	5.33	3.40	3.90	4.22	3.69	3.99

SOURCE: California Employment Department, *Socio-Economic Trends in California, 1940–1980* (Sacramento, 1986), p. 17.
NOTE: Latino defined as Spanish surname.

TABLE A.2
Total and Age-Specific Fertility Rates, California, 1980

Age group	Anglo	Black	Asian	Latino U.S.-born	Latino Foreign-born
Total rate	*1.31*	*1.70*	*1.59*	*2.06*	*3.14*
15–19	0.14	0.33	0.17	0.34	0.62
20–24	0.39	0.57	0.35	0.69	0.94
25–29	0.43	0.47	0.53	0.54	0.72
30–34	0.27	0.25	0.36	0.34	0.52
35–39	0.08	0.08	0.15	0.09	0.26
40–44	0.01	0.02	0.03	0.05	0.09

SOURCE: U.S. Bureau of the Census, *Census of Population and Housing, 1980: Public Use Microdata Sample A, California* (Washington, D.C., 1983).
NOTE: The *Anglo* fertility rates do not include Latinos. Thus, they are lower than the frequently cited *White* fertility rates, which do include Latinos.

156   *Appendix*

year old in the same census data set. In other words, applying the fertility rates shown in Table A.2 to the appropriate number of women in the age-ethnicity-nativity cohort results in the number of zero-year-old children reported in the 1980 census.

There are two important qualifications that must be stated regarding the derivation of the fertility rates used in our projections. First, rather than representing the actual fertility experiences of a cohort of women who have completed their fertility, these rates are based on the simultaneous fertility of different age cohorts of women. Thus the actual total completed fertility of the younger cohorts could be different from the total fertility rate shown here. If this were to happen, the age-specific fertility rates of women over 30 would have to show a marked increase in the future. We assume that the age pattern of fertility will remain the same as it was in 1980.

The other qualification regarding our fertility rates is that they were calculated from census rather than vital registration data. Generally, registration data are preferred, but they have questionable accuracy for ethnic identification. This is even more true for the determination of ethnic- and nativity-specific fertility rates. There are problems inherent in calculating fertility rates from census data, specifically underenumeration and infant mortality. These problems are much more important in less-developed countries than in California (see Shyrock & Siegel 1975: Chap. 17).

In sum, we believe that our fertility rates give the most accurate picture available for ethnic and nativity differences in fertility. We assume that the age structure of fertility rates will remain the same. It may have been possible to derive more accurate estimates of fertility in 1980 by adjusting our rates for infant mortality, underenumeration, etc. However, given that the focus of our analysis is on the *future* of California's population trends, these efforts did not seem necessary or warranted. Our baseline projection results are within the fairly narrow results of other projections published since we began our work.

Mortality

The age-sex-ethnic specific mortality rates used in our projections were based on those published in "California Life Expectancy" (CDHS 1983a). These rates were used directly in the projections that assumed no future life-expectancy increase. The cohort-specific mortality rates for projections assuming five- and ten-year longevity increases were derived by decreasing each age-sex-ethnic-specific mortality rate by an equal proportion. The magnitude of this proportion was iteratively determined by varying the mortality rates and then calculating the life expectancy implied by these rates (Shyrock & Siegel 1975: Chap. 15). Therefore, the projections based on the assumption of increased longevity preserve existing sex and ethnic life span differences. Also implicit in this method is the assumption that the age pattern of mortality will remain stable.

Any reasonable alternative method and set assumptions would make only trivial differences to our projection results.

Immigration

Our baseline net immigration estimates were developed by analyzing the change in population by age cohort and ethnicity between the 1970 and 1980 censuses. Estimates of the number of immigrant children aged 0 to 9 years are based on the number of children in families who were reported to have migrated to California since 1975, as indicated from tabulations of the 1 percent 1980 PUMS data. The resulting distributions are shown in Table A.3.

Although many factors might change the age, ethnic, and sex distributions of migrants in the future, our projections assume that current trends will continue: a similar ratio of males to females among Anglos and Blacks; a higher ratio of males to females among Asians; a higher ratio of males to females among Latinos; and a much older age structure among Asians than in other groups.

Immigration is the wild-card factor in any projection involving Latinos and other Third World populations. We alter this variable in three ways: (1) Latino immigration remains at a constant 100,000 per year; (2) there is a sudden influx, a sharp, discontinuous "spike" in Latino immigration leading to a 10-year increase from 1990 to 1999, then reverting back to the "normal" 100,000 per year; and (3) all foreign immigration ceases from 1985 onward, from all sources—Latin America, Asia, Africa, and Europe. As we note throughout this book, we consider a shut-off of immigration at any point unlikely. However, for this study, we arbitrarily chose to date this last assumption from 1985, the starting year of all our projections.

Several other researchers have made projections of the likely ethnic mix in California by 2000. Table A.4 shows how our baseline projections compare with three of those studies: the Population Research Unit of the California Department of Finance (CDOF), the Center for Continuing Study of the California Economy (CCSCE), and the Population Reference Bureau (PRB). The total population projections are quite similar, with a range of 31.4 million to 32.2 million in the year 2000. There are many reasons for differences in the various projections. Our base year is 1985; in the other studies the base year is 1980. Other differences are due to different assumptions, different methods, or different data bases. For example, our race/ethnic fertility rates were based on an analysis of the PUMS microdata for California; the PRB used national fertility rates, and the CDOF based its fertility rates on California Department of Health Services data. The CDOF based its total population projection on previously published projections, using its own ethnic-specific models to get cohort shares. In a somewhat similar manner, the CCSCE first projects total jobs, and then adjusts population levels to conform to the target number

Distribution of Baseline Annual Net Migration to California
by Ethnicity, Sex, and Age
(250,000 migrants)

Age group	Anglo (n = 75,000)		Black (n = 20,000)	
	Male	Female	Male	Female
Total	37,580	37,420	10,000	10,000
0–4	2,000	2,000	1,140	1,140
5–9	2,000	2,000	1,140	1,140
10–14	2,260	2,000	1,260	1,260
15–19	3,780	2,650	1,330	1,330
20–24	8,760	8,010	1,630	1,630
25–29	8,780	10,330	1,330	1,330
30–34	6,470	7,310	1,280	1,280
35–39	2,650	2,050	550	550
40–44	610	1,070	340	340
45–49				
50–54				
55–59				
60–64				
65–69				
70–74				
75–79				
80 & up				

Age group	Asian (n = 55,000)		Latino (n = 100,000)	
	Male	Female	Male	Female
Total	24,940	30,060	55,670	44,330
0–4	1,990	1,990	5,650	5,650
5–9	1,990	1,990	5,130	5,130
10–14	2,130	2,020	4,610	4,930
15–19	2,420	2,370	6,940	5,180
20–24	2,930	3,140	12,280	9,010
25–29	3,190	4,320	11,120	8,420
30–34	3,210	4,310	7,700	4,610
35–39	2,050	2,420	2,110	1,400
40–44	1,450	1,680	130	
45–49	1,020	1,330		
50–54	760	1,030		
55–59	590	1,020		
60–64	550	960		
65–69	510	860		
70–74	150	480		
75–79		140		
80 & up				

SOURCE: Same as Table A.2.

TABLE A.4
Comparison of Selected Population Projections, California, 2000
(Population in millions)

Study	Anglo	Black	Asian	Latino	Total
Model baseline	17.94	2.63	2.98	8.68	32.23
CDOF	16.84	2.49	3.72	8.36	31.41
CCSCE high	17.44	2.25	3.19	8.93	31.81
CCSCE low	18.34	2.39	3.10	7.71	31.54
PRB	16.70	2.35	3.74	9.09	31.88

NOTE: CDOF is California Department of Finance, *Projected Total Population for California by Race/Ethnicity* (Sacramento, 1986); CCSCE is Center for Continuing Study of the California Economy, *Projections of Hispanic Population for California, 1985–2000* (Palo Alto, Calif., 1982); PRB is Population Reference Bureau, *Population Change and California's Future* (Washington, D.C., 1985).

of jobs. Our study is unique in differentiating the Latino population into the U.S.-born and the foreign-born. It also investigates a greater number of contingencies than the others; the CDOF and the PRB studies are both limited to one analysis, and the CCSCE study explores only two alternatives.

Projections of Labor Force and Income

It is unclear to what degree migration generates employment by producing an abundant supply of labor, as opposed to the demand for labor generating an influx of migrants. Overall both processes are continually at work. Certainly the population movement that brought numbers of Vietnamese to the state in the 1980's, for example, was not initiated because of a particularly great demand for labor. On the other hand, Mexico and much of Central America have chronic conditions of surplus labor with unemployment rates of 40 percent and higher. The earnings differential between Mexico and the United States is the largest for any two contiguous nations in the world. Labor market and economic differentials are central to the motivation for much Latino in-migration.

Our forecasts show that California's population will grow at a slower rate than hitherto. Furthermore, the Baby Boom generation has already been absorbed in the labor force and the percent of the population of working age is projected to decline by 2030 under all simulations (Table A.5). For these reasons, our projections of labor force and income are directly derived from our population projections. Each projected age-sex-ethnicity-nativity cohort population has been multiplied by the corresponding projected labor-force participation rate to estimate future labor-force size.

The changing picture of labor-force participation between 1940 and 1980 is shown in Table A.6. In general, the male labor-force participation

TABLE A.5

Population Projections by Age and Ethnicity, California, 1985–2030

(Population in millions)

Category	1985	2000	2015	2030
Total	*26.22*	*32.24*	*37.39*	*41.58*
Youth	5.86	6.24	6.32	6.34
Working age	17.48	21.94	25.37	25.94
Elderly	2.88	4.06	5.70	9.29
Anglo	16.77	17.94	18.26	17.98
Black	2.04	2.63	3.17	3.64
Asian	1.83	2.98	4.12	5.19
Latino	5.58	8.68	11.84	14.76
Anglo				
Youth	3.02	2.65	2.25	1.97
Working age	11.36	12.26	12.24	10.59
Elderly	2.39	3.04	3.78	5.43
Black				
Youth	0.55	0.61	0.65	0.68
Working age	1.36	1.80	2.17	2.33
Elderly	0.13	0.22	0.34	0.62
Asian				
Youth	0.44	0.59	0.72	0.83
Working age	1.26	2.07	2.75	3.22
Elderly	0.13	0.32	0.66	1.15
Latino				
Youth	1.85	2.39	2.71	2.87
Working age	3.51	5.82	8.20	9.80
Elderly	0.22	0.48	0.92	2.09

NOTE: Youth is defined as 0–15 years, working age as 16–64 years, and elderly as 65 and over in this and subsequent tables. Columns may not sum because of rounding.

TABLE A.6

Labor-Force Participation Rates by Sex and Ethnicity, California, 1940–1980

(Percent of working-age population in labor force)

Category	1940	1950	1960	1970	1980
Male total	*82.6%*	*83.6%*	*81.4%*	*76.6%*	*76.1%*
Anglo	82.6	83.5	81.2	76.9	76.2
Black	82.4	84.2	79.4	70.5	66.7
Asian	81.7	80.2	83.2	74.1	74.8
Latino	83.8	85.7	83.7	78.4	80.6
Female total	*27.9%*	*29.1%*	*37.1%*	*42.2%*	*52.5%*
Anglo	27.8	28.5	36.8	41.8	51.7
Black	43.4	40.5	46.8	48.6	55.3
Asian	31.9	35.2	40.7	49.3	58.4
Latino	21.6	27.6	33.3	39.4	52.0

SOURCE: California Employment Development Department, *Socio-Economic Trends in California, 1940–1980* (Sacramento, 1986), p. 42.
NOTE: Latino defined as Spanish surname.

rate (labor force divided by working-age population for a group expressed as a percent) has fallen 6.5 points over the period, ranging from a drop of 3.2 points for Latinos to a drop of 15.7 points for Blacks. The trend among women has been just the opposite. Their participation rate has tended to climb steadily, with an overall jump of 24.6 points over 40 years, to reach 52.5 percent in 1980. Black women, who had much the highest level at the start of the period, have shown the smallest gain, 11.9 points; Latino women, starting from the lowest level of participation, have shown the largest growth, gaining 30.4 points.

Labor-force participation rates for 1980 by age, sex, ethnicity, and nativity are shown in Table A.7. Of particular note here is the sharp drop-off in participation between the 60–64 and 65–69 cohorts, reflecting the normal tendency to retire at about age 65. Since our main concern was the burden of support for the elderly, we made a separate economic simulation of the effect of delaying retirement for five years by substituting the labor-force participation rates of the 60–64 cohorts for the 65–69 rates.

Since the labor-force participation rates of Table A.7 are derived from the 1980 census, we updated the figures for our simulations with data from the Current Population Survey (CPS) for California as prepared by the Bureau of Labor Statistics. This updating process revealed significant drops between 1980 and 1985 in the participation rates of youth aged 16 to 19 and people 65 and older. These are shown in Table A.8. Also shown in Table A.8 are our baseline labor-force participation rates by age and sex for 1985 and the projected rates for 2030. The projections reflect historical changes revealed in the 1940–80 California data; projections of labor-force participation rates for the United States made by the Bureau of Labor Statistics; and refinements based on recent trends discernible in the updated 1985 data. The participation rates of youth aged 16–19 are projected to remain stable over the forecast period; those of the retirement group aged 65 and over to decline significantly; those of men to continue declining moderately; and those of women to continue increasing moderately.

The PUMS data provided detailed income information on individuals by income source. For our analysis we combined the census categories Wage and Salary Income, Nonfarm Self-Employment Income, and Farm Self-Employment Income, all of which are mostly tied to current work efforts, into a general category, Work Income. A second income category embraces Interest, Dividends, and Rent (IDR). These three kinds of income tend to be related primarily to prior investments, although rental income in some instances is derived from a person's work as a landlord. The most important question concerning IDR income is whether it can grow at rates far exceeding those of work income. Today's retirement plans are based on such expectations. Our final category, Unearned Income, comprises the census categories Social Security Income, Public Assistance Income, and All Other Income. Distinction between "earned" Social Security income and other forms of unearned income is blurred.

TABLE A.7
Labor-Force Participation Rates by Age, Sex, Ethnicity, and Nativity, California, 1980
(Percent of cohort in labor force)

Age group	Anglo		Black		Asian		Latino U.S.-born		Latino Foreign-born	
	Male	Female	Male	Female	Male	Female	Male	Female	Male	Female
16–19	73.8%	68.9%	48.1%	43.7%	62.2%	56.3%	61.1%	53.2%	67.2%	49.5%
20–24	93.4	85.0	83.6	71.5	81.1	75.8	90.5	77.2	89.2	63.9
25–29	95.4	78.0	87.1	78.1	89.7	75.7	91.9	72.1	92.5	62.4
30–34	95.9	73.5	88.1	78.0	91.5	72.9	93.5	70.6	94.7	63.2
35–39	96.3	72.8	89.2	76.3	95.8	68.3	95.2	66.8	94.6	61.3
40–44	95.4	73.4	87.3	73.6	95.0	75.3	93.5	64.3	91.5	59.9
45–49	94.3	68.5	82.1	66.7	94.0	74.0	90.0	63.3	90.0	57.5
50–54	91.5	61.5	76.7	58.5	90.6	62.4	85.7	56.8	87.7	60.4
55–59	83.4	53.2	65.2	48.0	85.2	56.0	79.2	47.5	80.7	46.5
60–64	68.6	41.2	54.7	35.8	81.8	40.5	64.9	33.2	72.7	29.7
65–69	38.7	18.2	22.6	19.4	45.6	19.2	25.4	15.4	37.3	14.9
70–74	23.0	10.3	15.5	8.8	28.8	14.0	20.3	6.9	15.5	8.3
75–79	15.1	5.3	7.8	10.3	13.8	10.4	3.4	6.1	13.5	5.6
80–84	9.0	4.0	17.2	3.5	3.3	5.9	18.2	4.2	8.9	1.4
85–89	6.5	2.5	7.7	12.5	12.5	0.0	9.1	4.8	9.5	0.0
90 & up	4.8	3.4	25.0	0.0	0.0	0.0	25.0	16.7	11.1	0.0

SOURCE: U.S. Bureau of the Census, *Census of Population and Housing, 1980: Public Use Microdata Sample A, California* (Washington, D.C., 1983).

TABLE A.8

Labor-Force Participation Rate Projections by Age and Sex, California, 2030

(Percent)

Category	1980: CPS	1985: CPS	1985: Baseline (model)	2030: model
Male				
16–19	66.7%	54.5%	55.2%	55.2%
20–24	87.5	85.6	88.8	84.6
25–34	94.2	94.1	94.0	84.6
35–44	96.1	94.2	93.0	83.7
45–54	92.5	90.3	89.1	75.7
55–64	71.5	65.6	69.1	55.2
65 & up	17.5	15.5	21.5	9.7
Female				
16–19	54.3%	48.3%	53.9%	53.9%
20–24	70.3	69.6	78.9	86.8
25–34	66.4	70.4	78.3	90.0
35–44	69.4	71.7	73.7	84.8
45–54	60.4	64.9	69.1	79.5
55–64	40.3	42.5	48.6	53.5
65 & up	7.8	6.7	8.6	3.9

SOURCE: CPS rates, U.S. Department of Labor, *Current Population Survey*, 1980–85 reports.

The 1980 per-capita income data for California were updated to 1985 on the basis of published national data (*Survey of Current Business*, selected issues, 1980–85). The 1985 baseline figures, broken down by age, sex, ethnicity, and nativity, are shown in Tables A.9–A.12.

As illustrated in Table A.9, there are large differences across age-sex-ethnicity-nativity groups. Anglo males in the prime working ages of 25 to 64 outearn all other groups, and in most cases by substantial amounts. There is also a consistent male-female gap in all categories, but this is partially explained by the lower labor-force participation of women. And we see another large and consistent difference in earnings between U.S.-born and foreign-born Latinos. The gap between Anglos and other groups is even wider in the case of IDR income, as shown in Table A.10. As would be expected, this category of income tends to be highest in the older cohorts. The high costs of retirement programs can be appreciated in Table A.11, indicated by the high unearned income per capita in the 65 and older cohorts.

Total per-capita income (Table A.12) is the sum of work, IDR, and unearned income. It might seem reasonable to assume that the income gaps between Anglo males and other groups will close by the year 2030, and indeed this could happen. But such a development would run against

(*Text continued on p. 168*)

TABLE A.9
Per-Capita Work Income by Age, Sex, Ethnicity, and Nativity, California, 1985
(Dollars per year)

Age group	Anglo Male	Anglo Female	Black Male	Black Female	Asian Male	Asian Female	Latino U.S.-born Male	Latino U.S.-born Female	Latino Foreign-born Male	Latino Foreign-born Female
16–19	$3,135	$2,281	$1,768	$1,387	$2,247	$1,796	$2,501	$1,853	$3,701	$1,907
20–24	11,126	7,143	7,345	4,912	7,380	5,770	9,906	6,018	8,411	4,542
25–29	19,005	9,431	12,638	9,024	14,529	8,832	15,414	7,615	12,224	4,873
30–34	25,456	9,985	16,619	10,947	20,163	10,382	20,340	7,789	14,751	5,430
35–39	31,957	10,232	18,416	10,973	25,675	9,525	23,556	7,586	16,678	6,028
40–44	33,362	10,319	20,206	10,754	25,649	10,466	23,396	6,888	16,132	5,408
45–49	33,574	9,879	19,811	8,935	27,195	9,894	22,872	7,156	16,394	5,035
50–54	31,139	8,815	18,851	8,061	24,248	8,476	19,325	5,428	16,174	5,656
55–59	27,064	7,826	14,543	5,566	22,956	6,121	18,398	5,349	14,476	4,842
60–64	20,668	5,422	10,374	4,033	19,112	4,897	13,640	3,178	11,022	2,358
65–69	7,998	1,801	2,762	2,276	7,819	1,320	4,393	918	5,089	890
70–74	4,268	929	1,690	687	3,096	1,256	3,130	790	1,309	567
75–79	2,618	458	1,039	1,620	2,318	318	33	505	1,659	236
80–84	2,302	510	1,925	417	202	227	3,289	689	406	108
85–89	1,139	270	433	9	0	0	1,898	274	2,074	0
90 & up	728	291	1,063	0	0	0	4,139	296	3,119	0

SOURCE: U.S. Bureau of the Census, Census of Population and Housing, 1980: Public Use Microdata Sample A, California (Washington, D.C., 1983). NOTE: "Work Income" equals the census categories Wage and Salary Income, Nonfarm Self-Employment Income, and Farm Self-Employment Income.

TABLE A.10
Per-Capita Interest, Dividend, and Rental Income by Age, Sex, Ethnicity, and Nativity, California, 1985
(Dollars per year)

Age group	Anglo		Black		Asian		Latino U.S.-born		Latino Foreign-born	
	Male	Female	Male	Female	Male	Female	Male	Female	Male	Female
16–19	$126	$134	$3	$14	$85	$116	$10	$21	$11	$26
20–24	190	121	57	13	189	140	132	32	43	25
25–29	461	272	308	57	286	171	170	25	119	81
30–34	819	382	123	53	800	186	170	90	154	42
35–39	1,369	558	213	153	1,090	334	378	67	331	25
40–44	2,134	642	391	140	1,263	620	676	129	226	65
45–49	2,464	827	1,223	202	2,493	454	787	261	306	228
50–54	3,395	1,302	317	520	2,706	977	844	284	523	213
55–59	4,570	1,752	655	225	3,151	1,005	893	427	913	166
60–64	5,519	2,749	611	223	3,159	1,881	2,716	932	897	632
65–69	7,588	3,302	447	476	2,903	1,035	1,840	596	1,517	631
70–74	7,888	4,429	447	332	2,232	1,528	2,225	1,814	1,904	454
75–79	7,612	4,542	1,118	192	2,974	2,086	416	388	1,271	1,283
80–84	8,698	3,945	1,074	928	3,172	1,758	102	3,286	828	1,042
85–89	8,013	4,763	377	1,688	152	2,413	0	2,000	1,112	1,244
90 & up	5,617	3,743	0	147	3,438	526	0	121	0	125

SOURCE: Same as Table A.9.

TABLE A.11
Per-Capita Unearned Income by Age, Sex, Ethnicity, and Nativity, California, 1985
(Dollars per year)

Age group	Anglo		Black		Asian		Latino U.S.-born		Latino Foreign-born	
	Male	Female	Male	Female	Male	Female	Male	Female	Male	Female
16–19	$376	$432	$414	$813	$483	$409	$307	$472	$230	$426
20–24	444	504	619	1,680	681	535	375	835	300	387
25–29	522	610	912	1,655	591	645	643	1,033	441	338
30–34	574	730	913	1,790	443	578	827	1,090	474	598
35–39	557	939	1,141	1,700	500	604	573	1,264	608	918
40–44	990	812	1,327	1,538	602	590	862	1,409	591	851
45–49	1,349	862	2,116	1,854	925	436	1,229	907	799	1,143
50–54	1,820	917	2,613	2,185	967	886	1,878	1,082	1,262	984
55–59	3,269	1,236	3,543	2,078	2,005	1,111	2,908	1,314	1,838	1,307
60–64	5,781	2,766	4,695	3,517	2,245	1,567	3,981	2,443	2,298	2,098
65–69	9,926	5,351	7,915	5,590	5,667	3,545	8,332	5,008	7,036	3,908
70–74	9,919	5,877	8,249	6,365	6,875	4,087	8,175	5,685	7,364	4,598
75–79	8,805	6,094	8,895	5,319	7,098	4,217	7,556	5,726	7,242	5,274
80–84	8,878	5,434	7,120	4,650	5,387	4,352	4,907	5,446	6,403	4,590
85–89	7,722	5,037	5,242	4,802	7,651	4,322	5,565	5,122	4,959	4,452
90 & up	6,199	3,981	6,517	4,131	4,503	4,664	7,025	3,386	3,808	5,123

SOURCE: Same as Table A.9.
NOTE: "Unearned Income" equals the census categories Social Security Income, Public Assistance Income, and All Other Income.

Total Per-Capita Income by Age, Sex, Ethnicity, and Nativity, California, 1985

Age group	Anglo		Black		Asian		Latino			
							U.S.-born		Foreign-born	
	Male	Female	Male	Female	Male	Female	Male	Female	Male	Female
16–19	$3,637	$2,847	$2,185	$2,213	$2,816	$2,321	$2,817	$2,346	$3,942	$2,359
20–24	11,760	7,768	8,021	6,605	8,749	6,645	10,413	6,886	8,753	4,954
25–29	19,988	10,313	13,858	10,736	15,406	9,648	16,227	8,673	12,784	5,292
30–34	26,849	11,097	17,655	12,791	21,406	11,146	21,337	8,969	15,379	6,070
35–39	33,883	11,729	19,771	12,826	27,264	10,464	24,506	8,917	17,617	6,971
40–44	36,486	11,773	21,924	12,432	27,513	11,675	24,934	8,426	16,949	6,325
45–49	37,386	11,568	23,150	10,991	30,613	10,784	24,888	8,325	17,498	6,406
50–54	36,354	11,033	21,481	10,767	27,921	10,339	22,046	6,794	17,959	6,853
55–59	34,902	10,818	18,741	7,870	28,112	8,238	22,199	7,089	17,227	6,315
60–64	31,968	10,937	15,680	7,774	24,517	8,345	20,336	6,553	14,217	5,088
65–69	25,512	10,424	11,125	8,342	16,389	5,900	14,564	6,522	13,642	5,430
70–74	22,074	11,236	10,386	7,384	12,203	6,871	13,530	8,290	10,577	5,619
75–79	19,035	11,094	11,052	7,132	12,389	6,621	8,004	6,620	10,172	6,793
80–84	19,878	9,889	10,119	5,995	8,761	6,338	8,298	9,421	7,637	5,741
85–89	16,873	10,070	6,052	6,499	7,803	6,735	7,462	7,396	8,144	5,696
90 & up	12,544	8,015	7,580	4,278	7,941	5,190	11,190	3,806	6,928	5,248

SOURCE: Same as Table A.9.

168   *Appendix*

TABLE A.13
Annual Earnings of Persons Aged 25–64 by Sex and Ethnicity,
California, 1940–1980
(Constant 1972 dollars)

Category	1940	1950	1960	1970	1980
Total all groups	$3,040	$3,850	$5,450	$7,040	$6,840
Male total	$3,370	$4,570	$6,710	$8,930	$8,710
Anglo	3,520	4,790	7,090	9,470	9,560
Black	1,980	3,240	4,490	6,150	6,590
Asian	1,680	2,930	4,960	7,320	7,350
Latino	2,000	3,330	5,060	6,670	6,130
Female total	$2,100	$2,220	$3,140	$4,110	$4,410
Anglo	2,170	2,280	3,280	4,260	4,550
Black	1,250	1,830	2,260	3,660	4,650
Asian	1,290	2,290	2,560	4,070	4,470
Latino	1,340	1,830	2,440	3,150	3,370

SOURCE: California Employment Development Department, *Socio-Economic Trends in California, 1940–1980* (Sacramento, 1986), p. 58.
NOTE: Latino defined as Spanish surname.

the California experience of the last 40 years: income gaps have persisted on a percentage basis and grown on a constant dollar basis. Table A.13 shows constant dollar earnings for people aged 25 to 64 by sex and ethnicity from 1940 to 1980. Only two groups have made significant progress in closing the gap with Anglo males—Black women and Asian men. In both cases these gains were coincident with major shifts in occupation. In 1940 80 percent of Black women worked in services, primarily as household domestics; by 1980 the proportion had dropped to 22 percent. Over 44 percent of Asian males were farmworkers in 1940; the figure had dropped to under 3 percent by 1980.

In our baseline model we have assumed that real income in 1985 constant dollars will grow by 1 percent a year in the period 1985–2030. As a growth rate that is about 50 percent higher than the rate for 1970–85 but lower than the rate for 1950–70, we feel this level is a reasonable basis for analysis. We have included two other simulations, both at higher growth rates, although we do not consider either very likely: a "high productivity" rate of 1.5 percent a year, which compounded over 45 years results in about 2.50 times the growth that would be achieved from the 1 percent growth rate, and a "very high productivity" rate of 2.0 percent, which would raise the compounding effect to 3.75.

When projecting income, in addition to the 1 percent annual real growth rate, we made different assumptions depending on the type of income under consideration. Work income by age-sex-ethnicity-nativity cohort was projected to change proportionately with the number of

TABLE A.14
Population, Labor Force, and Income by Age Group and Ethnicity, California, 1985

Category	Popula-tion	Labor force	Earned income	IDR income	Unearned income	Total income
Total	26.22	13.98	$251.08	$30.46	$38.59	$320.04
Youth	5.86	0.00	0.00	0.00	0.00	0.00
Working age	17.48	13.58	243.99	16.47	18.62	279.07
Elderly	2.88	0.40	7.09	13.99	19.97	40.97
Anglo	16.77	9.36	185.93	27.85	29.90	243.67
Black	2.04	1.00	14.19	0.35	2.98	17.51
Asian	1.83	1.00	16.49	1.26	1.57	19.28
Latino	5.58	2.63	34.47	1.00	4.14	39.57
Anglo						
Youth	3.02	0.00	0.00	0.00	0.00	0.00
Working age	11.36	9.02	179.00	14.45	12.76	206.95
Elderly	2.39	0.33	6.19	13.40	17.13	36.72
Black						
Youth	0.55	0.00	0.00	0.00	0.00	0.00
Working age	1.36	0.98	13.98	0.28	2.11	16.36
Elderly	0.13	0.02	0.21	0.07	0.87	1.15
Asian						
Youth	0.44	0.00	0.00	0.00	0.00	0.00
Working age	1.26	0.97	16.14	0.99	0.90	18.04
Elderly	0.13	0.03	0.35	0.27	0.67	1.25
Latino						
Youth	1.85	0.00	0.00	0.00	0.00	0.00
Working age	3.51	2.61	34.13	0.74	2.85	37.72
Elderly	0.22	0.03	0.34	0.26	1.30	1.85

NOTE: In this table and the others that follow, population and labor force are in millions, income is in billions of 1985 dollars.

people in the labor force in that cohort. Thus, increasing labor-force participation rates translates into larger earned incomes for the cohort, and conversely for decreasing labor-force participation rates. IDR income by age-sex-ethnicity-nativity cohort was projected to grow by the number of people in the cohort regardless of their labor-market status. Finally, unearned income was projected to change in proportion to the number of people not in the labor force, this based on the fact that most unearned income goes to either prime-age people who are not working or people who are past the normal working age and retired.

The results of our simulations are shown in the accompanying tables. Table A.14 presents our baseline data for 1985. Tables A.15–A.25 give our simulation projections for 2030 under various alternative assumptions.

Since these simulations are discussed in detail in the text, we will limit our remarks here to the basic area of our concern. Tables A.14 and A.15 lay out the burden-of-support issue. The elderly population is expected to grow almost fourfold (388 percent) between 1985 and 2030, while the labor force grows by only about 40 percent. Real work income, which includes a 1 percent per annum growth factor reflecting expected education and technological enhancements, increases by 114 percent over the 45-year period. Currently, seniors receive $40.97 billion, which is shared by 2.88 million persons for a per-capita total income from all sources of $14,226. If all types of per-capita income increase by the same 1 percent per year, the total income of the elderly will increase to $175.15 billion by 2030 (all dollar amounts are in 1985 dollars). This would be shared by 9.29 million people, for a per-capita income of $18,854, a rise of $4,628 from 1985.

However, society may not be willing or able to finance this greater burden and, for example, senior income may only grow in the aggregate at the rate of work income. If this were the case, only $86.42 billion would be available for the elderly in 2030; each senior would then receive on average $9,303, and under this condition of proportionate real growth, the living standard of the elderly would be a third higher than the level in 1985. Should their total income grow in proportion to work income, their living standard would be two-thirds of the 1985 level.

As indicated, we see the first condition as a maximum upper bound on elderly income that is possible but unlikely, and the second as a minimum lower bound that is also possible but unlikely. Whether one or the other, or something in between, obtains only time will tell. What is certain is that policies of the next 10 to 15 years will dramatically affect the standard of living and social conditions of all Americans after 2010. The trade-offs need to be understood and decisions made now to provide for a better and more secure future.

TABLE A.15

Population, Labor Force, and Income by Age Group and Ethnicity,
California, 2030, Baseline Assumptions

Category	Popula-tion	Labor force	Earned income	IDR income	Unearned income	Total income
Total	41.58	19.82	$536.93	$96.22	$172.75	$803.96
Youth	6.34	0.00	0.00	0.00	0.00	0.00
Working age	25.94	19.28	523.13	39.09	66.50	628.81
Elderly	9.29	0.54	13.80	57.14	106.15	175.15
Anglo	17.98	8.40	270.48	76.82	101.03	448.34
Black	3.64	1.68	39.52	1.55	13.63	54.58
Asian	5.19	2.52	66.60	8.98	15.79	90.05
Latino	14.76	7.22	160.33	8.88	42.30	210.98
Anglo						
Youth	1.97	0.00	0.00	0.00	0.00	0.00
Working age	10.59	8.09	261.28	27.75	33.34	322.36
Elderly	5.43	0.31	9.20	49.07	67.70	125.97
Black						
Youth	0.68	0.00	0.00	0.00	0.00	0.00
Working age	2.33	1.65	38.86	0.99	6.78	46.63
Elderly	0.62	0.03	0.66	0.55	6.85	7.95
Asian						
Youth	0.83	0.00	0.00	0.00	0.00	0.00
Working age	3.22	2.44	65.10	5.38	5.67	76.14
Elderly	1.15	0.08	1.50	3.60	10.12	13.91
Latino						
Youth	2.87	0.00	0.00	0.00	0.00	0.00
Working age	9.80	7.10	157.89	4.96	20.81	183.67
Elderly	2.09	0.12	2.44	3.91	21.48	27.37

NOTE: Assumptions are baseline population; labor-force participation as in Table A.8; real income growth of 1 percent per annum.

TABLE A.16
Population, Labor Force, and Income by Age Group and Ethnicity,
California, 2030, Delayed Retirement Assumptions

Category	Popula-tion	Labor force	Earned income	IDR income	Unearned income	Total income
Total	41.58	20.76	$566.84	$93.75	$157.11	$815.75
Youth	6.34	0.00	0.00	0.00	0.00	0.00
Working age	25.94	19.28	523.13	39.09	66.60	628.81
Elderly	9.29	1.48	43.71	54.67	90.51	186.94
Anglo	17.98	8.92	289.68	74.05	92.13	455.85
Black	3.64	1.75	41.09	1.53	12.67	55.18
Asian	5.19	2.64	70.27	9.24	14.29	92.50
Latino	14.76	7.45	165.79	8.93	38.20	212.23
Anglo						
Youth	1.97	0.00	0.00	0.00	0.00	0.00
Working age	10.59	8.09	261.28	27.75	33.34	322.36
Elderly	5.43	0.84	28.40	46.30	58.79	133.49
Black						
Youth	0.68	0.00	0.00	0.00	0.00	0.00
Working age	2.33	1.65	38.86	0.99	6.78	46.63
Elderly	0.62	0.10	2.23	0.54	5.89	8.54
Asian						
Youth	0.83	0.00	0.00	0.00	0.00	0.00
Working age	3.22	2.44	65.10	5.38	5.67	76.14
Elderly	1.15	0.20	5.18	3.86	8.63	16.35
Latino						
Youth	2.87	0.00	0.00	0.00	0.00	0.00
Working age	9.80	7.10	157.89	4.96	20.81	183.67
Elderly	2.09	0.35	7.90	3.97	17.21	28.56

NOTE: Assumptions are same as Baseline (Table A.15) except the labor-force participation and per-capita income of the 65–69 cohort are set to the values of the 60–64 cohort by sex, ethnicity, and nativity.

TABLE A.17
Population, Labor Force, and Income by Age Group and Ethnicity,
California, 2030, High Achievement Assumption

Category	Popula-tion	Labor force	Earned income	IDR income	Unearned income	Total income
Total	41.58	20.45	$897.97	$200.55	$276.15	$1,374.96
Youth	6.34	0.00	0.00	0.00	0.00	0.00
Working age	25.94	19.66	870.14	87.53	122.52	1,080.19
Elderly	9.29	0.80	27.83	113.02	153.63	294.48
Anglo	17.98	8.83	378.24	105.41	143.15	626.80
Black	3.64	1.83	78.66	15.00	20.99	114.66
Asian	5.19	2.53	111.34	24.84	33.96	170.14
Latino	14.76	7.71	329.73	55.29	78.05	463.07
Anglo						
Youth	1.97	0.00	0.00	0.00	0.00	0.00
Working age	10.59	7.93	362.52	39.29	54.21	456.03
Elderly	5.43	0.45	15.72	66.13	88.93	170.78
Black						
Youth	0.68	0.00	0.00	0.00	0.00	0.00
Working age	2.33	1.77	76.68	7.43	10.52	94.63
Elderly	0.62	0.06	1.98	7.57	10.48	20.03
Asian						
Youth	0.83	0.00	0.00	0.00	0.00	0.00
Working age	3.22	2.44	108.04	10.93	15.27	134.23
Elderly	1.15	0.09	3.30	13.91	18.69	35.91
Latino						
Youth	2.87	0.00	0.00	0.00	0.00	0.00
Working age	9.80	7.52	322.89	29.88	42.52	395.30
Elderly	2.09	0.20	6.83	25.41	35.53	67.77

NOTE: Assumptions are baseline population; all other sex-ethnicity-nativity cohorts achieving same levels of labor-force participation and income as those of Anglo males.

TABLE A.18

Population, Labor Force, and Income by Age Group and Ethnicity,
California, 2030, Latino Influx Assumption

Category	Population	Labor force	Earned income	IDR income	Unearned income	Total income
Total	49.08	23.53	$620.47	$100.53	$193.73	$912.79
Youth	7.82	0.00	0.00	0.00	0.00	0.00
Working age	31.11	22.91	605.17	41.78	78.32	725.27
Elderly	10.16	0.62	15.31	58.75	115.40	187.52
Anglo	17.98	8.40	270.48	76.82	101.03	448.34
Black	3.64	1.68	39.52	1.55	13.63	54.58
Asian	5.19	2.52	66.60	8.98	15.79	90.06
Latino	22.27	10.93	243.87	13.19	63.28	319.81
Anglo						
Youth	1.97	0.00	0.00	0.00	0.00	0.00
Working age	10.59	8.09	261.28	27.75	33.34	322.36
Elderly	5.43	0.31	9.20	49.07	67.70	125.97
Black						
Youth	0.68	0.00	0.00	0.00	0.00	0.00
Working age	2.33	1.65	38.86	0.99	6.78	46.63
Elderly	0.62	0.03	0.66	0.55	6.85	7.95
Asian						
Youth	0.83	0.00	0.00	0.00	0.00	0.00
Working age	3.22	2.44	65.10	5.38	5.67	76.14
Elderly	1.15	0.08	1.50	3.60	10.12	13.91
Latino						
Youth	4.34	0.00	0.00	0.00	0.00	0.00
Working age	14.97	10.73	239.93	7.66	32.54	280.13
Elderly	2.96	0.19	3.94	5.53	30.73	39.69

NOTE: Assumptions are Latino net immigration of 100,000 a year except for 1990–99, when the annual figure jumps to 500,000, in population projections; all other immigration, labor-force, and income assumptions as in baseline.

TABLE A.19
Population, Labor Force, and Income by Age Group and Ethnicity,
California, 2030, No Foreign Immigration Assumption

Category	Popula-tion	Labor force	Earned income	IDR income	Unearned income	Total income
Total	32.66	15.05	$430.52	$89.68	$155.23	$673.87
Youth	4.88	0.00	0.00	0.00	0.00	0.00
Working age	19.55	14.56	417.77	34.29	55.32	507.38
Elderly	8.63	0.49	12.75	55.39	99.91	166.49
Anglo	17.98	8.40	270.48	76.82	101.03	448.34
Black	3.64	1.68	39.52	1.55	13.63	54.58
Asian	2.17	0.92	25.04	4.46	8.64	37.22
Latino	8.87	4.04	95.48	6.85	31.92	133.73
Anglo						
Youth	1.97	0.00	0.00	0.00	0.00	0.00
Working age	10.59	8.09	261.28	27.75	33.34	322.36
Elderly	5.43	0.31	9.20	49.07	67.70	125.97
Black						
Youth	0.68	0.00	0.00	0.00	0.00	0.00
Working age	2.33	1.65	38.86	0.99	6.78	46.63
Elderly	0.62	0.03	0.66	0.55	6.85	7.95
Asian						
Youth	0.28	0.00	0.00	0.00	0.00	0.00
Working age	1.17	0.88	24.18	2.17	2.27	28.62
Elderly	0.72	0.05	0.86	2.29	6.37	8.60
Latino						
Youth	1.56	0.00	0.00	0.00	0.00	0.00
Working age	5.46	3.94	93.45	3.37	12.93	109.76
Elderly	1.86	0.10	2.03	3.48	18.99	23.97

NOTE: Assumptions are no foreign immigration from 1985 on in population projections; baseline labor-force and income assumptions.

TABLE A.20
Population, Labor Force, and Income by Age Group and Ethnicity,
California, 2030, Low Fertility Assumption

Category	Population	Labor force	Earned income	IDR income	Unearned income	Total income
Total	37.84	18.27	$504.86	$95.75	$169.88	$768.56
Youth	4.62	0.00	0.00	0.00	0.00	0.00
Working age	23.92	17.73	491.06	38.62	63.73	593.41
Elderly	9.29	0.54	13.80	57.14	106.15	175.15
Anglo	17.98	8.40	270.48	76.82	101.03	448.34
Black	3.20	1.52	36.27	1.51	13.27	50.94
Asian	4.86	2.39	64.00	8.89	15.63	87.20
Latino	11.80	5.96	134.12	8.53	39.95	182.08
Anglo						
Youth	1.97	0.00	0.00	0.00	0.00	0.00
Working age	10.59	8.09	261.28	27.75	33.34	322.36
Elderly	5.43	0.31	9.20	49.07	67.70	125.97
Black						
Youth	0.47	0.00	0.00	0.00	0.00	0.00
Working age	2.11	1.49	35.61	0.96	6.42	42.99
Elderly	0.62	0.03	0.66	0.55	6.85	7.95
Asian						
Youth	0.65	0.00	0.00	0.00	0.00	0.00
Working age	3.06	2.32	62.49	5.29	5.50	73.29
Elderly	1.15	0.08	1.50	3.60	10.12	13.91
Latino						
Youth	1.54	0.00	0.00	0.00	0.00	0.00
Working age	8.17	5.84	131.68	4.62	18.47	154.77
Elderly	2.09	0.12	2.44	3.91	21.48	27.32

NOTE: Assumptions are all ethnic groups at Anglo 1985 fertility level by 2000 in population projections; baseline labor-force and income assumptions.

TABLE A.21
Population, Labor Force, and Income by Age Group and Ethnicity,
California, 2030, High Life Expectancy Assumption

Category	Population	Labor force	Earned income	IDR income	Unearned income	Total income
Total	43.09	20.06	$544.85	$105.27	$187.65	$835.31
Youth	6.36	0.00	0.00	0.00	0.00	0.00
Working age	26.23	19.47	529.64	39.87	67.96	637.47
Elderly	10.50	0.60	15.21	65.40	119.68	197.84
Anglo	18.89	8.52	275.01	84.92	111.00	470.93
Black	3.79	1.72	40.39	1.68	15.03	56.94
Asian	5.30	2.53	66.95	9.30	16.63	91.26
Latino	15.11	7.30	162.50	9.36	44.99	216.17
Anglo						
Youth	1.97	0.00	0.00	0.00	0.00	0.00
Working age	10.72	8.17	264.81	28.35	34.08	327.24
Elderly	6.20	0.35	10.20	56.57	76.92	143.69
Black						
Youth	0.69	0.00	0.00	0.00	0.00	0.00
Working age	2.37	1.68	39.65	1.02	7.00	47.67
Elderly	0.73	0.04	0.75	0.66	8.02	9.27
Asian						
Youth	0.83	0.00	0.00	0.00	0.00	0.00
Working age	3.23	2.45	65.39	5.42	5.71	76.52
Elderly	1.23	0.08	1.56	3.88	10.92	14.74
Latino						
Youth	2.88	0.00	0.00	0.00	0.00	0.00
Working age	9.91	7.17	159.79	5.07	21.17	186.04
Elderly	2.33	0.13	2.70	4.29	23.81	30.14

NOTE: Assumptions are 10-year increase in life expectancy in population projections; baseline labor-force and income assumptions.

TABLE A.22
Population, Labor Force, and Income by Age Group and Ethnicity,
California, 2030, Low Life Expectancy Assumption

Category	Population	Labor force	Earned income	IDR income	Unearned income	Total income
Total	39.89	19.52	$527.25	$86.37	$156.31	$768.50
Youth	6.32	0.00	0.00	0.00	0.00	0.00
Working age	25.58	19.04	515.02	38.11	64.91	618.03
Elderly	7.99	0.48	12.23	48.26	91.40	150.47
Anglo	16.99	8.26	264.96	68.07	90.11	423.14
Black	3.46	1.65	38.45	1.40	12.12	51.91
Asian	5.07	2.50	66.16	8.60	14.82	88.59
Latino	14.37	7.12	157.67	8.30	39.25	204.86
Anglo						
Youth	1.96	0.00	0.00	0.00	0.00	0.00
Working age	10.43	7.98	256.88	27.00	32.41	316.29
Elderly	4.60	0.28	8.08	41.07	57.70	106.85
Black						
Youth	0.68	0.00	0.00	0.00	0.00	0.00
Working age	2.27	1.62	37.89	0.96	6.51	45.35
Elderly	0.51	0.03	0.56	0.44	5.62	6.55
Asian						
Youth	0.82	0.00	0.00	0.00	0.00	0.00
Working age	3.20	2.43	64.72	5.33	5.61	75.67
Elderly	1.04	0.07	1.43	3.27	9.21	12.92
Latino						
Youth	2.86	0.00	0.00	0.00	0.00	0.00
Working age	9.68	7.01	155.52	4.83	20.37	180.72
Elderly	1.83	0.11	2.16	3.47	18.88	24.14

NOTE: Assumptions are no increase in life expectancy in population projections; baseline labor force and income projections.

TABLE A.23

Population, Labor Force, and Income by Age Group and Ethnicity,
California, 2030, No Productivity Increase Assumption

Category	Popula-tion	Labor force	Earned income	IDR income	Unearned income	Total income
Total	41.58	19.82	$343.13	$61.49	$110.40	$513.77
Youth	6.34	0.00	0.00	0.00	0.00	0.00
Working age	25.94	19.28	334.31	24.98	42.56	401.84
Elderly	9.29	0.54	8.82	36.51	67.84	111.93
Anglo	17.98	8.40	172.85	49.09	64.57	286.51
Black	3.64	1.68	25.25	0.99	8.71	34.88
Asian	5.19	2.52	42.56	5.74	10.09	57.55
Latino	14.76	7.22	102.46	5.67	27.03	134.83
Anglo						
Youth	1.97	0.00	0.00	0.00	0.00	0.00
Working age	10.59	8.09	166.97	17.73	21.30	206.01
Elderly	5.43	0.31	5.88	31.36	43.26	80.50
Black						
Youth	0.68	0.00	0.00	0.00	0.00	0.00
Working age	2.33	1.65	24.83	0.63	4.33	29.80
Elderly	0.62	0.03	0.42	0.35	4.38	5.08
Asian						
Youth	0.83	0.00	0.00	0.00	0.00	0.00
Working age	3.22	2.44	41.60	3.44	3.62	48.66
Elderly	1.15	0.08	0.96	2.30	6.47	8.89
Latino						
Youth	2.87	0.00	0.00	0.00	0.00	0.00
Working age	9.80	7.10	100.90	3.17	13.30	117.37
Elderly	2.09	0.12	1.56	2.50	13.73	17.46

NOTE: Assumptions are baseline population with baseline labor-force assumptions, but no per-capita income growth.

TABLE A.24
Population, Labor Force, and Income by Age Group and Ethnicity,
California, 2030, High Productivity Increase Assumption

Category	Popula-tion	Labor force	Earned income	IDR income	Unearned income	Total income
Total	41.58	19.82	$670.55	$120.17	$215.74	$1,004.03
Youth	6.34	0.00	0.00	0.00	0.00	0.00
Working age	25.94	19.28	653.31	48.81	83.17	785.29
Elderly	9.29	0.54	17.24	71.35	132.57	218.73
Anglo	17.98	8.40	337.79	95.94	126.17	559.90
Black	3.64	1.68	49.35	1.93	17.02	68.17
Asian	5.19	2.52	83.17	11.21	19.72	112.47
Latino	14.76	7.22	200.23	11.08	52.82	263.49
Anglo						
Youth	1.97	0.00	0.00	0.00	0.00	0.00
Working age	10.59	8.09	326.30	34.65	41.63	402.58
Elderly	5.43	0.31	11.49	61.28	84.54	157.32
Black						
Youth	0.68	0.00	0.00	0.00	0.00	0.00
Working age	2.33	1.65	48.53	1.24	8.47	58.24
Elderly	0.62	0.03	0.82	0.69	8.56	9.93
Asian						
Youth	0.83	0.00	0.00	0.00	0.00	0.00
Working age	3.22	2.44	81.30	6.72	7.08	95.09
Elderly	1.15	0.08	1.87	4.49	12.64	17.37
Latino						
Youth	2.87	0.00	0.00	0.00	0.00	0.00
Working age	9.80	7.10	197.18	6.20	25.99	229.37
Elderly	2.09	0.12	3.05	4.89	26.83	34.11

NOTE: Assumptions are baseline population with baseline labor-force assumptions and income growth rate of 1.5 percent a year.

TABLE A.25
*Population, Labor Force, and Income by Age Group and Ethnicity,
California, 2030, Very High Productivity Increase Assumption*

Category	Popula-tion	Labor force	Earned income	IDR income	Unearned income	Total income
Total	41.58	19.82	$836.50	$149.91	$269.13	$1,252.51
Youth	6.34	0.00	0.00	0.00	0.00	0.00
Working age	25.94	19.28	814.99	60.89	103.75	979.64
Elderly	9.29	0.54	21.51	89.01	165.38	272.87
Anglo	17.98	8.40	421.39	119.68	157.40	698.47
Black	3.64	1.68	61.57	2.41	21.24	85.04
Asian	5.19	2.52	103.76	13.99	24.60	140.30
Latino	14.76	7.22	249.78	13.83	65.90	328.70
Anglo						
Youth	1.97	0.00	0.00	0.00	0.00	0.00
Working age	10.59	8.09	407.05	43.23	51.94	502.23
Elderly	5.43	0.31	14.34	76.45	105.47	196.26
Black						
Youth	0.68	0.00	0.00	0.00	0.00	0.00
Working age	2.33	1.65	60.54	1.55	10.56	72.65
Elderly	0.62	0.03	1.02	0.86	10.67	12.38
Asian						
Youth	0.83	0.00	0.00	0.00	0.00	0.00
Working age	3.22	2.44	101.42	8.38	8.83	118.63
Elderly	1.15	0.08	2.34	5.61	15.77	21.67
Latino						
Youth	2.87	0.00	0.00	0.00	0.00	0.00
Working age	9.80	7.10	245.98	7.73	32.43	286.14
Elderly	2.09	0.12	3.80	6.09	33.47	42.55

NOTE: Assumptions are same as high productivity (Table A.24), but with income growth rate of 2.0 percent a year.

References Cited

References Cited

No place of publication is given for California state government works (all published in Sacramento) or U.S. government works (Washington, D.C.). The following abbreviations are used in the text citations: CDHS, California Department of Health Services, Center for Health Statistics; EDD, California Employment Development Department; USBC, U.S. Bureau of the Census.

Anderson, Harry, with Gloria Barger, Mary Hager, and Howard Fineman. 1983. "The Social Security Crisis," *Newsweek*, Jan. 24: 18–28.

Anderson, Harry, with Mary Hager. 1981. "The Crisis in Social Security," *Newsweek*, June 1: 25–27.

Aranda, Robert G. 1971. "The Mexican American Syndrome," *American Journal of Public Health*, 61: 104–9.

Arce, Carlos H. 1982. "Language Proficiency and Other Correlates of Voting by Mexican Origin Citizens." Paper presented at the 10th Meeting of the National Association for Chicano Studies, Tempe, Ariz.

Berger, Peter L., and Thomas Luckmann. 1967. *The Social Construction of Reality: A Treatise in the Sociology of Knowledge.* New York.

Butz, William P., Kevin F. McCarthy, Peter A. Morrison, and Mary E. Vaiana. 1982. *Demographic Challenges in America's Future.* Santa Monica, Calif.

California, Assembly Office of Research. 1985. *Dropping Out, Losing Out: The High Cost for California.*

———, Department of Finance. 1983. *Population Projections for California Counties, 1980–2020.* Report 83 P-3.

———, ———. 1986. *Projected Total Population for California by Race/Ethnicity.* Report 86 P-4.

———, Department of Health Services, Center for Health Statistics. 1980. *Vital Statistics of California, 1979–80.*

———, ———. 1982. "Twenty Leading Causes of Death for California (All Races) and Ten Leading Causes of Death by Race and Spanish Origin, by Number and Rank, California, 1980," *Data Matters*, Sept.: 25.

186   *References Cited*

———, ———. 1983a. "California Life Expectancy: Abridged Life Tables for California and Los Angeles County, 1979–81," *Data Matters*, July: 16–17.

———, ———. 1983b. "Mortality in California, 1979–81: Leading Causes of Death by Sex and Age," *Data Matters and Topical Reports*.

———, ———. 1984a. "Death Rates by Age and Race/Ethnicity, California, 1979–81," *Public Health Dateline*, 4(12): 4.

———, ———. 1984b. "Health Status of Californians by Race/Ethnicity—1970 and 1980," *Data Matters and Topical Reports*.

———, Employment Development Department. 1981. *California Labor Market Issues: Hispanics*.

———, ———. 1986. *Socio-Economic Trends in California, 1940–1980*.

———, Office of Statewide Health Planning and Development. 1982. *EEO Special File: Detailed Occupational Categories by Race/Hispanic Origin and Sex*.

———, Postsecondary Education Commission. 1982. *California College-Going Rate. 1981 Update*.

———, ———. 1984. *Postsecondary Education in California, 1982 Information Digest*.

———, State Department of Education. 1981. *Racial/Ethnic Distribution of Staff and Students in California Public Schools*.

Campbell, Angus, Philip E. Converse, Warren E. Miller, and Donald E. Stokes. 1960. *The American Voter*. New York.

Carlson, Richard. 1982. "Threat to State's High Tech Leadership," *San Francisco Chronicle*, April 17.

Center for Continuing Study of the California Economy. 1982. *Projections of Hispanic Population for California, 1985–2000*. Palo Alto, Calif.

Chavez, Leo. 1985. "Use of Health Services by Undocumented Families in San Diego County." Paper presented at conference of the California Policy Seminar and the School of Social Welfare, University of California, Berkeley.

Colegio de Mexico, Centro de Estudios Economicos y Demograficos. 1970. *Dinamica de la Poblacion de Mexico*. Mexico, D.F.

Davis, Karen. 1983. "Association Testimony Urges Child Health Benefits," *The Nation's Health*, August.

Fonner, Edwin. 1975. "Mortality Differences of 1970 Texas Residents." Master's thesis, School of Public Health, University of Texas.

Gardner, David P. 1984. "Higher Education Holds Key to Future of California," *University Bulletin* 33(16): 1.

Gonzalez Meza, Choco. 1981. *The Latino Vote in the 1980 Presidential Election: A Political Research Report*. San Antonio, Tex. Published by Southwest Voter Registration Education Project.

Gordon, Milton M. 1964. *Assimilation in American Life*. New York.

Gruenberg, Ernest M. 1977. "The Failure of Success," *Milbank Memorial Fund Quarterly: Health and Society*, 55.

Guendelman, Sylvia, and Joan Schwalbe. 1986. "Medical Care Utilization by Hispanic Children: How Does It Differ from Black and White Peers?" *Medical Care*, 24(10).

Guernica, Antonio, and Irene Kasperuk. 1982. *Reaching the Hispanic Market Effectively*. New York.

Gwertzman, Bernard. 1985. "The Debt to the Indochinese Is Becoming a Fiscal Drain," *New York Times*, March 3.

Hayes-Bautista, David E., Werner Schink, and Jorge Chapa. 1982. *The Hispanic Portfolio*. Sacramento. Published by the California Hispanic Affairs Council.

Hayes-Bautista, David E., and Jorge Chapa. 1987. "Latino Terminology: Conceptual Bases for Standardized Terminology," *American Journal of Public Health*, 77(1): 61–68.

Hernandez, Andrew. 1977. *The Latino Vote in the 1976 Presidential Election*. San Antonio, Tex. Published by the Southwest Voter Registration Education Project.

Herring, Hubert. 1968. *A History of Latin America*. New York.

Hill, David B., and Norman P. Luttbeg. 1983. *Trends in American Electoral Behavior*. 2d ed. Itasca, Ill.

Hirschman, Albert O. 1970. *Exit, Voice and Loyalty: Responses to Declines in Firms, Organizations and States*. Cambridge, Mass.

Hobsbawm, Eric J. 1965. *Primitive Rebels: Studies in Archaic Forms of Social Movements in the 19th and 20th Centuries*. New York.

Hodgkinson, Harold. 1983. "Educating Minorities in Nation's Best Interest," *Equal Opportunity in Higher Education*, Dec. 12: 7–8.

Kaufman, Steve. 1982. "U.S. Firms Face Some Crying Needs Due to 'Baby Bust'," *San Jose Mercury*, Feb. 15.

Kelley, Eugene T. 1982. "America's Economic Future—The Key Is Brains and Services," *San Francisco Chronicle*, Dec. 16.

Keyfitz, Nathan. 1983. "Age, Work and Social Security," *Society*, July/August: 45–51.

Kimball, Larry J., David Hensley, and Iraj Heravi. 1986. "Towards a General Equilibrium Model of International Labor Migration." Paper presented at the 35th Annual UCLA Business Forecasting Conference, Graduate School of Management. December.

Kingson, Eric R., and Richard Scheffler. 1981. "Aging: Issues and Economic Trends for the 1980's," *Inquiry*, 18: 197–213.

Kramer, Morton. 1980. "The Rising Pandemic of Mental Disorders and Associated Chronic Diseases and Disorders," *Acta Psychiatrica Scandinavica*, supplement 285, vol. 62.

Lopez Acuna, Daniel. 1982. *La Salud Desigual en Mexico*. Mexico, D.F.

McCarthy, Kevin F. 1986. "What Are the Prospects for Immigration After Reform?" Paper presented at the 35th Annual UCLA Business Forecasting Conference, Graduate School of Management. December.

McCarthy, Kevin F., and Robert Valdez. 1985. *Current and Future Effects of*

Mexican Immigration in California. Executive Summary. Santa Monica, Calif.

Manton, Kenneth G. 1982. "Changing Concepts of Morbidity and Mortality in the Elderly Population," *Milbank Memorial Fund Quarterly: Health and Society*, 60(2): 183–244.

Menck, R., B. E. Henderson, M. C. Pike, T. Mack, S. P. Martin, and Soo Hoo. 1975. "Cancer Incidence in the Mexican American," *Journal of the National Cancer Institute*, 55: 531–36.

Mexican American Legal Defense and Education Fund (MALDEF). 1981. "Chicano Political Participation in the Southwest." San Francisco. Mimeo.

Mexico, Consejo Nacional de Poblacion. 1978. *Mexico Demografico.* Mexico, D.F.

——, ——. 1982. *Mexico: Estimaciones y Proyecciones de Poblacion, 1950–2000.* Mexico, D.F.

——, Instituto Mexicano de Seguro Social. 1984. *Jalisco: Diagnostico de Salud.* Guadalajara. Published by Servicios Coordinados de Jalisco.

Mondragon, Delfi. 1985. "Critical Care Patients with Low Probability of Survival: Clinical Correlations and Decision Making." Ph.D. dissertation, School of Public Health, University of California, Berkeley.

Montoya, Roberto, Edward Smelloff, Louis Gonzalez, and David E. Hayes-Bautista. 1978. "Minority Dental School Graduates," *American Journal of Public Health*, 68(1): 1017–19.

Nie, Norman, Sidney Verba, and John P. Petrocik. 1976. *The Changing American Voter.* Cambridge, Mass.

Novak, Michael. 1972. *The Rise of the Unmeltable Ethnics: Politics and Culture in the Seventies.* New York.

Omran, Abdel R. 1977. "Epidemiological Transition in the U.S.," *Population Bulletin*, 32(2): 15–21.

Petersen, Peter G. 1982a. "No More Free Lunch for the Middle Class," *New York Times Magazine*, Jan. 17.

Petersen, Peter G. 1982b. "Social Security: The Coming Crash," *New York Review of Books*, 29(19): 34–38.

Population Reference Bureau. 1985. *Population and California's Future.* Washington, D.C.

Portes, Alejandro, and Robert L. Bach. 1985. *Latin Journey.* Berkeley, Calif.

Pressat, Roland. 1985. *The Dictionary of Demography.* Oxford, Eng.

Preston, Samuel H. 1984. "Children and the Elderly in the U.S.," *Scientific American*, 251(6): 44–49.

Rice, Dorothy, and Jacob Feldman. 1982. "Demographic Changes and Health Needs of the Elderly." Paper presented at the meeting of the Institute of Medicine, Washington, D.C.

Riddell, Adaljizas. 1980. "Chicanos and Reapportionment in California." In Rose Institute of State and Local Government, *Chicano Politics and the California Redistricting*, pp. 8–32.

Rivas, Sergio. 1985. *Foro Mexico 2010: Escenarios economicos*. Mexico, D.F. Published by the Fundacion Javier Barros Sierra, A.C.

Roberts, Robert E., and Eun Sol Lee. 1980. "The Health of Mexican Americans: Evidence from the Human Population Laboratory Studies," *American Journal of Public Health*, 70(4): 375–80.

Rose Institute of State and Local Government. 1980. *Chicano Politics and the California Redistricting*. Pomona, Calif.

Rudov, Melvin, and Nancy Santangelo. 1979. *Health Status of Minorities and Low Income Groups*. U.S. Department of Health, Education, and Welfare publication no. 79–627.

Sanchez-Albornoz, Nicolas. 1974. *The Population of Latin America*. Berkeley, Calif.

Santillan, Richard. 1980. "California Reapportionment and the Chicano Community: An Historical Overview, 1960–1980." In Rose Institute of State and Local Government, *Chicano Politics and the California Redistricting*, pp. 51–96.

Scammon, Richard M., and Ben J. Wattenberg. 1971. *The Real Majority*. New York.

Schutz, Alfred. 1973. *Collected Papers, I: The Problem of Social Reality*. The Hague.

Shyrock, Henry S., and Jacob S. Siegel. 1975. *The Methods and Materials of Demography*. Washington, D.C.

Stanford University, Policy Analysis for California Education. 1984. *Condition of Education in California*. April.

Stern, Michael P., W. L. Haskell, P. O. S. Wood, K. E. Osau, A. B. King, and J. W. Farquhar. 1975. "Affluence and Cardiovascular Risk Factors in Mexican Americans and Other Whites in Three Northern California Communities," *Journal of Chronic Diseases*, 28: 623–36.

Turner, Caroline. 1984. "Demographic Shifts and Their Implications for Education: The Hispanic Population in California." In Stanford University, Policy Analysis for California Education, *Condition of Education in California*. April.

United Nations, Department of International Economic and Social Affairs. 1985. *Demographic Yearbook, 1983*. New York.

United States, Bureau of the Census. 1976. *Historical Statistics of the United States, Colonial Times to 1970*, part 1. Series A 119–34.

——, ——. 1979a. *Persons of Spanish Origin in the United States, March, 1979*. Current Population Reports, series P-20, no. 354.

——, ——. 1979b. *Voting and Registration in the Election of November, 1978*. Current Population Reports, series P-20, no. 355.

——, ——. 1980. *Ancestry and Language in the United States, November, 1979*. Current Population Reports, series P-23, no. 116.

——, ——. 1981. *Voting and Registration in the Election of November, 1980*. Current Population Reports, series P-20, no. 359.

——, ——. 1982a. *General Population Characteristics: California*, vol. 1, chapter B, part 6, PC80-1-B6.

——, ——. 1982b. *Persons of Spanish Origin by State, 1980.* PC80-S1-7.

——, ——. 1983a. *Voting and Registration in the Election of November, 1982.* Current Population Reports, series P-20, no. 383.

——, ——. 1983b. *Detailed Population Characteristics: California.* PC80-1-D6.

——, ——. 1983c. *Census of Population and Housing, 1980: Public Use Microdata Sample A, California.* Machine-readable data file.

——, ——. 1984. *Projections of the Population of the United States by Age, Sex, and Race: 1980 to 2030.* Current Population Reports, series P-25, no. 952.

——, ——. 1986a. *Statistical Abstract of the United States: 1985.*

——, ——. 1986b. *Projections of the Hispanic Population: 1983 to 2080.* Current Population Reports, series P-25, no. 995.

——, Health Resources and Services Administration. 1985. *Health Status of Minorities and Low Income Groups.* Department of Health and Human Resources, publication no. HRS-P-DU85-1.

——, Immigration and Naturalization Service. 1983. *Statistical Yearbook of the Immigration and Naturalization Service, 1981.*

——, National Center for Health Statistics. 1984. *Vital Statistics of the U.S., 1979.*

Urioste, Ricardo. 1982. *Anuario Mexicano, 1982.* Mexico, D.F.

Valdez, Armando, and Anthony Viera. 1983. "A Demographic Profile of Hispanics in the United States." Stanford University, Chicano Research Center. Mimeo.

Waterhouse, J., C. Muir, and C. Strangmugaratnawk, eds. 1982. *Cancer Incidence in Five Continents,* vol. 4. IARC Scientific Publication no. 42. Lyon.

Winslow, C. E., Wilson G. Smillie, James E. Doull, and John E. Gordon. 1952. *The History of American Epidemiology.* St. Louis, Mo.

Zazueta, Carlos H. 1980. "Mexican Workers in the United States: Some Initial Results and Methodological Considerations of the National Household Survey of Emigration." Working Group on Mexican Migrants and U.S. Reponsibility, Center for Philosophy and Public Policy, University of Maryland.

Zunzunegui, Victoria, Mary Claire King, C. F. Coria, and S. Charlett. 1985. "Husbands' Sexual Behavior and Cervical Cancer Risk Among Married Women in a Traditional Culture." School of Public Health, University of California, Berkeley. Mimeo.

Index

Index

Library of Congress Cataloging-in-Publication Data

Hayes-Bautista, David E., 1945–
    The burden of support.

    Bibliography: p.
    Includes index.
    1. Hispanic American youth—California—Social condi-
tions. 2. Hispanic American youth—California—Economic
conditions. 3. Hispanic Americans—California—Popula-
tion. 4. Demographic transition—California. I. Schink,
Werner O., 1945–   . II. Chapa, Jorge, 1953–   .
III. Title.
HQ796.H384   1988   305.2'35'08968720794   87-33564
ISBN 0-8047-1371-5 (alk. paper)
ISBN 0-8047-1802-4 (pbk)